ANGLISTIK UND ENGLISCHUNTERRICHT

Herausgegeben von
Gabriele Linke
Holger Rossow
Merle Tönnies

Band 82

NICOLE MARUO-SCHRÖDER
CHRISTOPH RIBBAT (Eds.)

Literature and Consumption in Nineteenth-Century America

Universitätsverlag
WINTER
Heidelberg

Bibliografische Information der Deutschen Nationalbibliothek

Die Deutsche Nationalbibliothek verzeichnet diese Publikation
in der Deutschen Nationalbibliografie;
detaillierte bibliografische Daten sind im Internet
über *http://dnb.d-nb.de* abrufbar.

Herausgeber:

Prof. Dr. Gabriele Linke
PD Dr. Holger Rossow
Prof. Dr. Merle Tönnies

ISBN 978-3-8253-6369-7
ISSN 0344-8266

Imprimé en Allemagne · Printed in Germany
Druck: Memminger MedienCentrum, 87700 Memmingen

Gedruckt auf umweltfreundlichem, chlorfrei gebleichtem
und alterungsbeständigem Papier

Den Verlag erreichen Sie im Internet unter:
www.winter-verlag.de

Contents

List of Illustrations

Nicole Maruo-Schröder (Koblenz-Landau)
Christoph Ribbat (Paderborn)

Introduction: Literature and Consumption in Nineteenth-Century America

1. More than Department Stores: Nineteenth-Century Consumer Culture

A hobby horse and a serial rifle, a pocket watch and a silver tea set: these are some of the nineteenth-century objects that recently turned into television protagonists. Every week, almost 10 million Americans watch *Antiques Roadshow*. They follow experts who appraise the value of century-old commodities. Apparently there is a lot of enthusiasm for this US spin-off of a BBC production, a show marketed as "[p]art adventure, part history lesson, and part treasure hunt."[1]

David Jaffee, an American material culture specialist, seems less passionate about the long-running program. To Jaffee, shows like *Antiques Roadshow* create a skewed picture of American consumption history, particularly where the nineteenth century is concerned. It is a mistake, he states, to imagine two distinct periods: the "emerging industrial colossus" of post-Civil War modern mass production on the one hand and the early nineteenth century with its artisanal objects on the other.[2] Industrial capitalism and other forms of production are "intimately connected," Jaffee proclaims. *A New Nation of Goods*, his study of early nineteenth-century craftsmen, proves his point. Whether producing clocks, chairs, or portraits, rural artisans worked in villages and took to the roads in order to provide consumers with commodities. They made objects that had once been luxury items available to small-town Americans with limited means. Jaffee depicts a "decentralized" world of manufacturing and consumption. However small its units, though, however close-knit its web, this system established the circulation that eventually turned the "middle-class parlor" into the center of domestic culture. It finally intensified in the second half of the nineteenth century, when industrialists created "a flood of fashionable cheap goods"[3]: consumer society proper.

Following some of David Jaffee's compelling observations, this volume aims to construct a more nuanced picture of the nineteenth century as a period of consumption – and as a period in which literary culture interacted with consumerism in a wide variety of fascinating ways. Until recently, the origins of contemporary consumer culture have routinely been located in the second half of the nineteenth century, more specifically in its last decades. The rise of the department store as well as the establishment of national consumer brands were taken to be signs and symptoms of a society that increasingly oriented itself towards consumption. Historian Charles McGovern defines the year 1890 as the starting point of the United States' transformation into a modern consumer society. In this period, Americans "learned to buy brand-name, trademarked commodities and to adopt new products and behaviors sold through a dizzying array of emporia and media."[4] As Kristin Hoganson shows, even the world of middle-class domesticity opened up to forms of globalized consumerism at the time. From imported products to French fashion trends to coverage in popular magazines, middle-class households turned into "contact zones" of consumerism, middle-class women into "world-class consumers."[5]

A larger framework reveals how consumption dominated the United States much earlier. Lawrence Glickman demonstrates that the "market revolution of the early nineteenth century," brought "mass-produced goods" first to middle-class customers in the cities, then to small towns. In a process beginning long before the first department store was ever planned, American ideas of what "necessities" were had begun to change. Even in the first decades of the nineteenth-century citizens had turned into consumers.[6] Antebellum America could still be described as an "economy of scarcity," as Kathleen McCarthy puts it.[7] Nonetheless, an infrastructure for commercial capitalism was already in place. By and by, American culture moved away from Puritan thrift.[8] And even rural antebellum Americans opened up to the "fancy goods" that David Jaffee evokes, sold to them not by national corporations but by "tinkerers [...] who travelled along dusty turnpikes." Nonetheless, these tinkerers were salesmen of products earlier generations had not felt the need for.[9]

Inspired by these new historical interpretations, this volume suggests a revised approach to the interactions between nineteenth-century literary texts and practices of consumption. If the markets of antebellum America and the 1890s were far more similar than observers once assumed, literary critics may also have to move away from overly neat categorizations. In order to gauge the function of literary texts in the consumer economy, we should read the realist and naturalist classics on late nineteenth-century American consumerism side by side with literary and popular texts exploring the flow of commodities five, six or even more decades before Theodore Dreiser portrayed department stores and Stephen Crane sketched spectacular bars. To highly specialized literary and cultural historians, the caesura of the Civil War may exert too much power. It is time, the editors propose, to reflect on shoppers and writers in a broader framework de-emphasizing overly strict definitions of literary and cultural periods.

This revised view of the nineteenth century also extends to the spaces of consumption and to communities shaped by commerce. As historians have shown, small-town and metropolitan consumer practices were much more similar than they seem at first glance. This observation should also prompt literary critics to operate with a more flexible picture of the spaces evoked by nineteenth-century authors reflecting on consumer practices. The new business of tourism, a focal point of this volume, exemplifies this flexibility. Our volume aims to challenge historical and spatial divisions taken for granted in superficial panoramas of the nineteenth century. What emerges is a multi-layered picture of readers, writers, and consumers as historical figures caught up in enormous transformations that shaped the entire century, not only the years following the Civil War. In order to paint this picture, one has to begin with the most obvious connection between the textual and the commercial aspects of this project: literature's function as a consumer object.

2. Literature and the Marketplace

Antebellum America, an age of "reading revolutions," saw an unprecedented proliferation of all kinds of printed material.[10] Books attained increasingly high status as consumer goods. They functioned as media for a wide number of purposes and topics and as 'mere' material, sometimes luxurious objects valued especially by the well-to-do. Literature responded to this new role in a variety of ways. Most Americans enthusiastically embraced the unprecedented availability of reading material. Others instructed readers on the values of consuming certain books and warned them about certain other types of literature. In *A Letter to Mothers* (1838), Lydia Huntley Sigourney admonished her (female) readers,

> though a taste for reading is an indication of mental health, [...] let no mother feel perfectly at ease about her children, simply *because they read*; unless she knows the characteristics of the books that engage their attention, and what use is made of the knowledge they impart.[11]

Stories abound of women who either read excessively or the wrong kind of literature. Caroline Kirkland's portrait of Elouise Fidler in *A New Home* (1838) is a case in point. Older than she cares to admit ("it must have taken a good while to read as many novels and commit to memory as much poetry, as lined the head and exalted the sensibilities of our fair visitant"), Elouise lives almost entirely in the fantasy world modeled on the hodgepodge of sentimental literature she has read. Now she is unfit for everyday life.[12] Literature, long fiction especially, took on new significance in discourses of moral education.[13]

Literary critics and cultural historians have paid close attention to literature's role in the nineteenth-century marketplace. The tremendous changes in the US economy had a major impact on literary developments. Some of these transformations, notably the rise of magazine culture, were directly related to the rapid growth of consumerism.[14] Technological advances in the area of paper production, printing, and binding (the development of the steam-driven cylinder press, the stereotyping of printing plates instead of assembling type by hand, bindings that were mass produced) made printing easier, quicker, cheaper, and more professionalized.[15] However, in contrast to mass-produced books available to many, 'exclusive' books, individually bound for their owners in bindings ranging from "cloth ($19.00)" to "morocco, super extra ($ 48.00)," formed another segment of the literary market. Some books served as "expensive luxury commodities well beyond the reach of most Americans."[16] Maybe even apart from the consumption of its contents, the book was considered a valuable commodity. It embodied a form of 'cultural capital' that could operate quite independently from literature's artistic contents.[17] A concomitant process placed a new focus on the importance of education and, more specifically, the development of an ideology linking "literacy, citizenship, and socialization."[18] A better infrastructure facilitated the distribution of all kinds of literature. New and extended shipping routes and railroad lines soon connected the large commercial and literary centers (such as Philadelphia and New York City) to the rest of the nation and thus a much larger audience.[19] The publishing business professionalized. This ended a period when books had been sold where they were printed so that, as Bell points out, "a popular book would often be available at only one store even in a large city."[20] The publishing industry also profited from the expansion and higher quality of school and college education. This led to an over-all increase in literacy. Public libraries provided access for those who could not buy books.[21] As the middle classes – and the numbers of those who aspired to belong to them – grew in size, more Americans spent money on books and time reading, which in and of itself became a sign of class distinction. Finally, the new technologies and quicker distribution processes made reading more affordable and hence more of an everyday activity than it had been before.

Other factors affecting the publishing industry came from the legal arena. They included the 1794 introduction of a special shipping rate for magazines. This led to an explosion of magazine publishing and hence shaped the development of literature, providing on the one hand more venues for publication and, on the other hand, creating the need for specific literary forms such as the sketch or the serialized novel.[22] Many magazines began to target specific audiences (e.g., women, religious groups, abolitionists) and thus also became outlets for texts of a specific ideological content geared to these reading publics. In 1790, the American copyright law had been passed, one of the most important factors in the professionalization of the writer. As William Charvat puts it, "law had given products of the mind the status of *property*," a clear indication that the literary market became increasingly commercialized.[23] In many ways, copyright law expressed in legal terms what the literary market slowly developed in practice, namely the notion that artistic creation and economic value could indeed go hand in hand.[24]

The commercialization and professionalization of the publishing industry enabled writers to live off their pens. But Americans regarded the professional author in ambivalent terms. Due to earlier notions of the 'gentlemanly writer,' taking on writing as a profitable business was, of course, problematic.[25] Moreover, writing itself, 'unproductive' as it was in a literal sense, was sometimes regarded as idleness. Such negative evaluations increased with certain genres. Prose was considered to be much less prestigious than history and poetry.[26] Pursuing writing as a full-time profession, therefore, seemed a paradox, given its associations with aristocratic leisure. Lawrence Buell identifies another contradiction: "The vocations both of full-time 'serious' artist and full-time 'commercial' artist were beginning to loom up as real possibilities for those without independent incomes, and with this came also a new ideological polarization."[27] While Henry David Thoreau set a record in producing eight drafts for *Walden*, emphasizing the artistic nature and literary quality of his text and his ambitions, other writers such as Sarah J. Hale were much more business-minded.[28]

For many of the era's authors, the line between artistic aspirations and commercial objectives became increasingly blurred. Thus, the first decades of the nineteenth century saw the birth of the professional author, notably in the figures of Washington Irving and James Fenimore Cooper.[29] Both struggled to remain successful and earn enough money with their writing, especially in their later years. But they set examples for others to follow. It continued to be difficult to rely on writing as one's sole financial source – Nathaniel Hawthorne, Herman Melville, and Edgar Allan Poe come to mind. But literature was now more frequently pursued as a career. Ironically, women, for whom it was not considered proper to work for money, became more and more successful competitors in the literary marketplace, particularly toward mid-century.

Even more than their male counterparts, women writers inhabited an ambiguous position. As 'true women' they were supposed to limit themselves to the private sphere. Home was their 'natural' realm, their sphere of influence. The fact that female writers entered the public sphere and earned money – and some of them fame – with their writing did not sit well with the ideology of 'true womanhood.'[30] Among other things, the writers' focus on the domestic and the sentimental novel – the 'home' and the field of emotion supposedly being the realms of their expertise – might have constituted one strategy to circumnavigate the problem. Routine modesty regarding their own literary achievements, as both Michael Davitt Bell and Susan Coultrap-McQuinn point out, surely was another.[31] Sara Payson Willis Parton's *Ruth Hall* (1855) elucidates the problems that female writers struggled with. Based on Parton's own life story and published under her pen name Fanny Fern, the novel shows how the widowed heroine turns to the pen and successfully earns a living for her family with her writing, in the process depicting literature as a marketable consumer good. Telling the success story it was eventually to become, the book caused a sensation (and subsequently became a best-seller) when Parton's true identity was revealed. She was chastised for her negative portrayal of her own family – not because readers thought it was untrue but because they deemed such criticism improper for a woman.[32]

The possibility to earn a living with the pen made both male and female professional authors more dependent on popularity and sales success and thus pressured them to conform to the aesthetic and ethic taste of the masses.[33] As literature became a commodity, authors' claims to artistic quality had to be reconciled with the tastes of their potential audiences. Financial success rather than artistic merit (in and of itself a rather vague if not arbitrary concept) came to be a criterion for the evaluation of literature.[34] At the same time, the didactic and moral aspects of literature continued to be important. They were intricately intertwined with popularity or success. This was particularly significant for women writers.[35] How seriously readers took this issue can be gleaned from ongoing discussions about the negative influence certain types of literature were said to have especially on young women's minds. As Buell points out, focusing on their readers' 'moral uplift' could also be a selling point for writers' works.[36] Breaching the (largely middle-class) norms and values of nineteenth-century society endangered one's literary career.

Numerous authors profited from the commercial opportunities presented to them. Others continued to struggle, either because they could not or would not write according to popular tastes. Henry David Thoreau's *Walden* (1854) presents an especially interesting example. The text critiques the growing consumer culture and its obsession with materialism. It also refuses to be categorized within any of the popular genres of its time. In many ways, it is an attack on a middle-class culture that increasingly relied on commodities to express its values. *Walden* opens with the warning that current consumer culture enslaves its participants in a vicious circle of consumption, so that most people are pressed to always earn (more) money in order to satisfy a growing desire for consumer goods they do not really need. In many ways, the text poses as a practical guide on how to do (better) with less. Lists that calculate income and expenditures seem to prove that this could be done. It is not surprising that nature and quasi-wilderness (together with Thoreau's simple, self-made cabin) are *Walden*'s main settings, providing an escape from a society obsessed with money and consumption. Against such materialism, Thoreau emphasizes the importance of people's spiritual and intellectual well-being, something that in his view money definitely cannot buy. Not without irony, he also reflects on the writer's need to sell his own products to an audience increasingly distracted by their focus on the purchase of material goods.[37] Pointedly, Thoreau refuses to write within any one genre. Drawing, among other things, on the adventure novel, nature writing, advice literature, the philosophical essay and even – in its focus on domestic issues – on the domestic novel, it disrupts and plays with literary conventions.[38] Judging from the modest sales of the book, the mass of American readers did not appreciate Thoreau's combination of literary innovation and social critique.[39] "Sell your clothes and keep your thoughts," *Walden* advises, nudging its readers to focus on intellectual rather than material wealth.[40] Even in Thoreau's lifetime, however, well before the age of brand names, department stores, and urban popular culture, "market considerations," as Michael Davitt Bell notes, had become "an inescapable component" of American literature.[41]

3. From Capitalist Excess to "Pious Consumption": Some Seminal Studies

Seminal works on nineteenth-century literature have emphasized the close relationship between markets and texts, literary and commodity culture. Methodological reflection is particularly pronounced in Walter Benn Michaels's *The Gold Standard and the Logic of Naturalism* (1987), a study that calls for a reconsideration of literature's role in capitalism. Michaels is interested in the way excess appears to "generate the power of both capitalism and the novel."[42] In Marxist terms, Michaels sees writing as remarkably similar to the commodity as a "thing whose identity involves more than its physical qualities."[43] In the same mode, literary production seems "neither material nor ideal." To Michaels, the late nineteenth-century American novel is just as much an actor within consumer capitalism as a reflective work of art.[44]

For an earlier, no less important literary movement of the nineteenth century, Michael Gilmore's *American Romanticism and the Marketplace* (1985) closely investigates the way a new market economy altered the literary sphere as much as all other arenas of American life. "[A]ll transactions," Gilmore argues, "including those between the author and his readers, were turned into money transactions."[45] No matter how harsh a given author's critique of the new commercial forces, the circulation of commodities and financial transactions: their "careers and art," Gilmore proclaims, "fought out [...] the question of the market's merits and liabilities."[46]

Along similar lines, Lori Merish's *Sentimental Materialism: Gender, Commodity Culture, and Nineteenth-Century American Literature* (2000) traces the ways in which literature throughout the nineteenth century partakes in the construction of "a modern consumer psychology" based on links between the culture of sentimentalism, (feminine) consumption and refinement.[47] Merish shows how "pious consumption" came to play a central role in middle-class ideology. Cherished "tasteful domestic objects were frequently described as 'spiritualizing,' 'civilizing,' and 'humanizing' the self, engaging an individual's sensibilities and 'refining' her emotional repertory."[48] Rather than being (luxury) objects that revealed an individual's selfishness and a distraction from God, commodities turned into tools for civilizing and improving oneself. Such a redefinition of consumption and ownership by the middle class, Merish argues, was not just an expression of class-based cultural ideologies. It helped to establish them as a general, 'national' standard.[49]

Focusing on the second half of the nineteenth century, Sarah Way Sherman's *Sacramental Shopping: Louisa May Alcott, Edith Wharton, and the Spirit of Modern Consumerism* (2013) explores how "issues of materialism, moral development, and self-construction" are negotiated by two authors who are usually not read side by side.[50] Sherman's concept of "sacramental shopping" reverberates with Merish's pious consumption in many ways. Sherman, too, analyzes how the middle class coped with the ever-growing importance of materialism and consumption by drawing on earlier religious discourses that tended to be suspicious of material wealth. Like Merish, Sherman emphasizes that such a redefinition of consumption became intricately intertwined with issues of gender and new ways of fashioning the self.

Babette Tischleder's *The Literary Life of Things: Case Studies in American Fiction* (2014) takes up the close connection between selfhood and the consumption of material objects.[51] While her study is more generally concerned with the ways objects are animated in literary texts, affecting their owners' lives in a variety of ways, Tischleder also focuses on the intersections of consumption and domesticity in texts from the second half of the nineteenth century. Taking Harriet Beecher Stowe's *House and Home Papers* as one of her examples, she argues that domestic objects become distinguished from objects of consumption through an explicitly 'female' caring for them. Objects that are thus animated almost become part of the family, as they function both as expressions of the housewife's character and sense of self and as tools in her attempt to civilize and socialize her family in an appropriate fashion.

Considering the important connections that these studies draw between middle-class culture and the growing influence of materialism, it is not surprising that bourgeois lifestyles and their literature went hand in hand with consumer goods and practices. Consumption did not just become an expression of middle-class culture. It turned into one of its constitutive elements and into an effective way of defining social status via distinctions drawn from both lower and upper classes. Nineteenth-century writers, many of whom were middle-class, frequently integrated such issues into their texts and reflected on the meaning of consumption and its moral and economic impact. Popular genres such as the domestic or sentimental novel were closely connected to consumption in a variety of ways. Not only were certain genres inherently well-suited to reflect on consumption but genre itself became a selling point. This many authors exploited successfully. As we will see in this volume, even those authors supposedly 'above' genre – Twain, James, Wharton and others – need to be read in conjunction with the history of consumption.

As Jonathan Arac demonstrates, the specific idea of what American literature constitutes is the result of a very long historical process. Broad late-eighteenth-century concepts treated philosophical and scientific, historical and travel writing as literature, drawing no lines between fiction and nonfiction. These conceptions developed into our contemporary, and much narrower, definitions of narrative literature as fiction, thus maintaining a safe distance to generic categories and conventions.[52] Nineteenth-century writers and the consumers of their texts played a part in this long history that redefined the role and cultural authority of literature in the national marketplace. The process accounts for the central role of commodities in novels, essays, and short fiction. As writers portrayed Americans and their close relationship with the commodities of everyday life, they also reflected on their own texts and their commercial potential. Hence, literary texts made for particularly charged arenas in which consumer capitalism was negotiated, in 1890s department stores and in antebellum cent shops.

4. What's On the Shelves: This Volume's Essays

Our volume opens with an analysis of a frequently neglected tradition in early American literature. Katja Kanzler's "Discourses of Production and Consumption in New England 'Factory Girl' Literature" engages with texts published in the *Lowell Offering* and written by women that were centrally involved in the production of nineteenth-century consumer goods: the women working in the textile mills of Lowell, Massachusetts. These writings have often been dismissed as aesthetically inferior and merely imitative of middle-class culture's literary taste, a perspective against which Kanzler undertakes a re-reading. Rather than trying to simply emulate "bourgeois ideas and conventions," Kanzler argues, 'factory girls' actively appropriated this culture to express and assert their own subject position in the complex economies of antebellum America. Consumption takes on a specific role in these texts. It serves as a mode to claim cultural equality with those historical figures whose cultural discourses often enough not only marginalized but even silenced and erased the vibrant culture of the textile mill workers.

In "A 'Dish Offered to the Public': The Business of Gender and Class in Nathaniel Hawthorne's *The House of the Seven Gables*," Nicole Maruo-Schröder focuses on the eponymous gothic house – a motif reverberating with the home as the key symbol of middle-class ideology – as the novel's central image. As her reading shows, Hawthorne functionalizes both the house and the cent shop inside to negotiate the changes that the rapid development of the capitalist marketplace brought to the U.S. While its two female inhabitants symbolize the gender and class changes that were part of this development, they also embody the new and changing roles of writers and readers during this time, thus linking economic transformations closely to the changes happening in the literary marketplace.

Christoph Ribbat's "'Where Do You Get Your Daguerreotypes?' Image, Text, Race, and a Nineteenth-Century Businessman" explores literary and pictorial commodities circulating in antebellum America, focusing on their specific significance in the central discourse of race. Exploring James Presley Ball, an African American photographer and author, Ribbat questions overly simplistic notions of nineteenth-century visual culture as per se racist. Daguerreotypes, key elements of visual culture, enabled black consumers to design and establish new public identities. Multimedia exhibitions (as produced by Ball in Cincinnati) constructed narratives of the African American experience that had been invisible up to the mid-nineteenth century. Thus, African American self-representation produced consumer objects and commercial cultural spectacles that challenged the dominant discourses of the antebellum years.

Klara Stephanie Szlezák also looks at literature and consumption from a multimedia perspective. Concord, Massachusetts, the geographical site and literary 'mecca' of New England, appears as a media ensemble in her essay. "Sages and Souvenirs: The Origins of American Literary Tourism in Concord, Massachusetts," carefully traces the town's many functions in establishing literary tourism as a collective practice. Concord, its writers, and the textual products of these authors were quickly commodified. Based on physical sites (museums, residences) and biographical and fictional sources, Szlezák's essay demonstrates how the middle ground between fictional production and an author's biography makes for a particularly rich area of cultural consumption.

Art Redding turns to another, related aspect of 'literary tourism' in his contribution "American Tourism and the Emergence of Mass Culture: Mark Twain's *The Innocents Abroad*." Tracing Twain's ambivalence about the emergence of American mass tourism (in the form of 'package tourism,' particularly to Europe), Redding shows how the author utilized and even commercially exploited his disdain for the 'tourist hordes' by satirizing them in his best-selling travelogue *The Innocents Abroad* (1869). Twain made fun of American mass tourism abroad. And yet, his work ultimately helped "to establish secure and productive class identities" that were so important for Americans in the second half of the nineteenth century.

Like Redding's, William Decker's essay zooms in on the intricate connections between realist fiction and commercialized tourism. "Consuming Europe: *Daisy Miller* and the Package Tour" discusses the ironic relationship of commodity culture and satiric representations, which turn into commodities themselves. Daisy Miller, James's charismatic protagonist, takes on iconic dimensions in Decker's piece. Advising us to "respect the currency with which she is abundantly endowed," Decker urges us to consider her as a substantial cultural figure oscillating between comedic lightness and intense spending power.

Simone Knewitz highlights another important aspect of the complex interconnections between literature and consumption. In her contribution "'Try My Tivoli': Conspicuous Consumption in William Dean Howell's *A*

Modern Instance," Knewitz argues that Howell's novel does more than critique the massive changes in America's public and private spheres under the growing influence of consumption. The text also partook in these transformations. Knewitz shows how the novel's ethics ultimately contradicts its aesthetics. Despite its association with moral deterioration and excess, consumption figures prominently in the novel as part of its realist agenda. Instead of depicting an alternative to commercial capitalism, *A Modern Instance* revels in the depiction of a spectacular world of consumption.

Eva Boesenberg's contribution "Sex and the City: Gender and Consumption in Late Nineteenth-Century Fiction" connects the sites and media of nineteenth-century consumption to contemporary shopping and its attendant representations. Boesenberg focuses on three texts on the tail end of the 'long nineteenth century,' Theodore Dreiser's *Sister Carrie* (1900), Paul Laurence Dunbar's *The Sport of the Gods* (1902) and Edith Wharton's *The Custom of the Country* (1903). She looks at the "purchasing possibilities" (Scanlon) of this period, unpacking the ambivalences of commodities and fictionalized women in the inner workings of an established gender order. In contrast to postmodern television series (*Sex and the City* serves as an example), Boesenberg argues for a reading of these texts that pays attention to their political potential, more liberating in the years before the First World War than in contemporary contexts of consumerism.

The "factory girls" explored in this collection's first essay thus turn into the metropolitan working women that move through its concluding study. Appropriately, these pieces frame the nineteenth century as a period in which texts, authors, and commodities circulated wildly, opening a host of perspectives on the dynamic relationship between the seemingly independent self and the omnipresent forces of the market. As the questions raised by these texts are more pressing than ever, the volume's editors hope that the case studies presented here will contribute to larger debates in the fields of literature, culture, and social history.

In conclusion, the editors would like to acknowledge the work of various colleagues and friends who have helped with this volume's production. Thus, we would like to thank the participants of the Paderborn conference "Buying America: Literature and Consumption in the Nineteenth Century," on which this collection is based, for exciting papers and lively discussions. No less important are those who helped us host this conference at the University of Paderborn in June 2012, most notably Esther Epp and Petra Tegtmeier. Alexander Dunst's comments on this introduction were extremely helpful, Julia Huneke and Julia Lünswilken helped us tirelessly and with attentive eyes to prepare the manuscript.

Notes

[1] "About Us." PBS/Antiques Roadshow Website. Posted 21 December, 2012. Web. 13 December 2013 <http://www.pbs.org/wgbh/roadshow/about.html>.
[2] David Jaffee (2011), *A New Nation of Goods: Artisans, Consumers, and Commodities in Early America, 1790-1860*. Philadelphia: University of Pennsylvania Press. ix.
[3] Jaffee (2011), xv.
[4] Charles F. McGovern (2006). *Sold American: Consumption and Citizenship, 1890 -1945*. Chapel Hill: University of North Carolina Press, 3.
[5] Kristin Hoganson (2007). *Consumer's Imperium: The Global Production of American Domesticity, 1865-1920*. Chapel Hill: University of North Carolina Press, 8; 255.
[6] Lawrence B. Glickman, Introduction. *Consumer Society in American History: A Reader*. Ed. L. B. G. Ithaca: Cornell University Press, 1999. 2 (1-14). See also T.H. Breen (2004), who argues that consumer goods and practices played a decisive role for the formation of America as a nation during the Revolution. Carole Shammas (1990) shows that pre-industrial America was far more dependent on consumption (and hence, less self-subsistent) than usually assumed.
[7] Kathleen D. McCarthy (2011), "Spreading the Gospel of Self-Denial: Thrift and Association in Antebellum America." *Thrift and Thriving in America: Capitalism and Moral Order from the Puritans to the Present*. Eds. Joshua J. Yates and James Davidson Hunter. Oxford: Oxford University Press. 178 (160-182).
[8] James Davidson Hunter and Joshua J. Yates (2011), "Introduction: Thrift and Thriving in America." *Thrift and Thriving in America: Capitalism and Moral Order from the Puritans to the Present*. Eds. J. J. Y. and J. D. H. Oxford: Oxford University Press, 13 (3-33).
[9] Jaffee (2011), xv.
[10] James L. Machor (2011), *Reading Fiction in Antebellum America: Informed Response and Reception Histories, 1820-1865*. Baltimore: Johns Hopkins University Press, 18.
[11] Lydia Huntley Sigourney (1838), "Letter XIII: Reading and Thinking." *Letters to Mothers*. Hartford: Hudson and Skinner. 148 (145-152). Emphasis in the original.

[12] Caroline Kirkland (1999 [1838]), *A New Home, Who'll Follow? Or Glimpses of Western Life.* Ed. Sandra A. Zagarell. New Brunswick: Rutgers University Press, 99; 100-107.

[13] Steven Mintz (1983), *A Prison of Expectations: The Family in Victorian Culture.* 23-24, qtd. in Lori Merish (2000), *Sentimental Materialism: Gender, Commodity Culture, and Nineteenth-Century American Literature.* Durham: Duke University Press, 118. See also Sarah Robbins (2004), especially the introduction (1-10) and chapter 1 (11-37).

[14] The basis for this summary and a concise overview over these changes is Michael Davitt Bell's (1995) "Conditions of Literary Vocation." *The Cambridge History of American Literature.* Vol 2: 1820-1865. Ed. Sacvan Bercovitch. Cambridge: Cambridge University Press, 9-123. An older but still classic reference point is William Charvat (1959). However, see also the more recent study by Leon Jackson (2007), in which he criticizes Charvat's notion of 'professionalization' as too one-dimensional for the antebellum period. Rather, Jackson argues, the "business of letters" (23) at that time consisted of a variety of economic practices much more complex than the simple notion of professionalization suggests. According to Jackson, even the 'early' literary market was not characterized by a clear distinction between amateurs and professional authors and the act of writing for money was often intricately intertwined with other activities, professions, and economies. Lawrence Buell's chapter on "Marketplace, Ethos, Practice: The Antebellum Literary Situation" (1986) constitutes an important reference point here: Buell focuses on the literary developments in New England. For a slightly different account see Ronald J. Zboray (1989), who emphasizes that it was not so much technological innovation (which did *not* make books affordable to everyone) that led to the growth of readership in antebellum America but other technologies that, among other things, "provided a new opportunity for reading, and helped to transform the nature of the reader's community life," notably the railroad (as new opportunity for reading), lighting technology (to provide light after work for reading), and eyesight correction (182). Zboray also provides a concise discussion of technological innovations and their impact on Americans' reading habits.

[15] Bell (1995), 16. Zboray (1989), however, cautions against "the easy equation of technological innovation in printing and the dramatic growth of the antebellum reading public" (181) and shows that book prizes by no means dropped so low as to be affordable by everybody. See Machor (2011) for a detailed argument that "the increased consumption of print in antebellum America did result from more people reading" (21).

[16] Ronald J. Zboray (1989) cites the range of Washington Irving's work as offered by George Putnam here. Like other items, books could be used to signal a certain class and status as they could "testif[y] to the owner's expensive taste in selecting fine commodities" (190).

[17] Zboray (1989) contends that "[t]he conspicuous consumption of books during

the era meant that some readers preferred owning books over reading them" (190). Nevertheless exclusive "bindings could enhance the experience of reading a much-beloved book" (190).

[18] Machor (2011), 23. See also Robbins (2004).

[19] See Machor (2011), chapter 1, who cautions that both increase in literacy and access to print material remained much more pronounced in urban America and did not necessarily extend to the whole nation at once.

[20] Bell (1995), 15.

[21] Machor (2011), 22.

[22] Bell (1995), 51.

[23] Charvat (1968), 6, emphasis in the original. International copyright was not enforced until 1891 (Bell 1995, 14). For a more detailed discussion of the impact of copyright see Charvat (1968), 31.

[24] Cathy N. Davidson (2004) points out that "[o]nce the product of the author's mind passes from idea to artifact and takes its form in the printed page, it necessarily becomes somebody's property and, as such, is subject to the same kinds of market conditions that govern the distribution of hogs or hog shares, patent medicines or blue-chip stocks, or any other commodity" (153).

[25] See Charvat (1968), who claims "that when the new nation began its career, its writers were thinking of the status of literature and authorship in terms of British aristocratic tradition, which was partly a myth" (6; cf. 7-8).

[26] Bell (1995), 17-18; see also Coultrap-McQuin (1990), especially chapter 2.

[27] Buell (1986), 59.

[28] *Ibid.*

[29] Bell (1995), 11, 17-37. As always, the notion of 'first' is problematic and in this case, it very much depends on the definition of what constitutes a 'professional author.' Charvat (1968) points out that Susannah Rowson, for instance, "is entitled to consideration as the first American professional writer of fiction" (20) since she was immensely prolific and professionally oriented as a writer. Frequently, Charles Brockden Brown is considered to be America's first professional author. For Charvat, both do not count since they did not exclusively support themselves by writing. Again, see Jackson (2008) for a nuanced discussion of 'professionalism' as an antebellum notion.

[30] See Mary Kelley (1984); Susan Coultrap-McQuin (1990), especially chapter 1.

[31] Bell (1995), 84; see also 81-82; Coultrap-McQuin (1990), 10-11.

[32] Joyce W. Warren (1986). Introduction. *Ruth Hall and Other Writings.* By Fanny Fern. Ed. J.W.W. New Brunswick: Rutgers University Press, ix, xvii (ix-xliii).

[33] However, one has to consider that in a system of patronage the dependence on the taste and preferences of the benefactor/ patron might have been a little less obvious but not necessarily less pressing. However, as literature begins to function as a commodity, the connection between literature and its financial value becomes even more obvious.

[34] The relation between popularity and artistic merit proves similarly awkward – see ongoing canon debates that often pass over the most popular authors of the nineteenth century.
[35] On the one hand, sensational works – frequently decried as indecent and hence, morally corrupting – were immensely successful and avidly read by many; on the other hand, publishers could and would reject texts they felt to be indecent for fear of loss of profit by alienating readers. Moreover, time and again authors have felt the consequences of writing about subject matters considered to be unacceptable and offensive. Cf. Charvat (1968), 19.
[36] Buell (1986), 63.
[37] See the famous basket episode, in which he compares a Native American's unsuccessful attempt to sell his woven basket to a lawyer (who does not see the need for it) to his own (failed) attempt to make his literary product "worth any one's while." Henry David Thoreau (1992 [1854]), *Walden and Resistance to Civil Government*. Ed. William Rossi. New York: Norton, 12.
[38] See Bell (1995), who points out that "[i]t is hard to imagine a book more sincerely domestic, both in its values and in its details, than Thoreau's *Walden*" (122). Bell finds the difference to more conventionally 'domestic' literature in the fact that *Walden*, like many other texts by male writers, reflects on "men who see themselves as fleeing the domestic or sentimental [but] are often simply running away from women to indulge their own version of domesticity and sentiment" (122).
[39] Yet, see also Richard Teichgraeber III (1995), who convincingly argues that despite the moderate sales of *Walden* both the author and the book were far from being overlooked in the literary scene of their day (see chapter 9).
[40] Thoreau (1992), 219.
[41] Bell (1995), 17.
[42] Walter Benn Michaels (1987), *The Gold Standard and the Logic of Naturalism: American Literature at the Turn of the Century*. Berkeley: University of California Press, 58.
[43] Michaels (1987), 21.
[44] *Ibid.*
[45] Michael T. Gilmore (1985), *American Romanticism and the Marketplace*. Chicago: University of Chicago Press, 4.
[46] Gilmore (1985), 8.
[47] Lori Merish (2000), 3.
[48] Merish (2000), 15. Merish borrows the term from Thomas Richards' study of commodity culture in Victorian England (fn 42).
[49] Merish (2000), 4, 8, 15-16.
[50] Sarah Way Sherman (2013), *Sacramental Shopping: Louisa May Alcott, Edith Wharton, and the Spirit of Modern Consumerism*. Durham: University of New Hampshire Press, 2.

[51] Babette B. Tischleder (2014). *The Literary Life of Things: Case Studies in American Fiction.* Frankfurt, New York: Campus.
[52] Jonathan Arac (1995), "Narrative Forms." *The Cambridge History of American Literature.* Vol 2: 1820-1865. Ed. Sacvan Bercovitch. Cambridge: Cambridge University Press, 608 (605-777).

Bibliography

"About Us." (2012) PBS/Antiques Roadshow Website. Posted 21 December, 2012. Web. 13 December 2013 <http://www.pbs.org/wgbh/roadshow/about.html>.

Arac, Jonathan (1995). "Narrative Forms." *The Cambridge History of American Literature.* Vol 2: 1820-1865. Ed. Sacvan Bercovitch. Cambridge: Cambridge University Press, 605-777.

Bell, Michael Davitt (1995). "Conditions of Literary Vocation." *The Cambridge History of American Literature.* Vol 2: 1820-1865. Ed. Sacvan Bercovitch. Cambridge: Cambridge University Press, 9-123.

Breen, T.H. (2004). *The Marketplace of Revolution: How Consumer Politics Shaped American Independence*. Oxford: Oxford University Press.

Buell, Lawrence (1986). *New England Literary Culture: From Revolution to Renaissance*. Cambridge: Cambridge University Press.

Charvat, William (1968). *The Profession of Authorship in America, 1800-1870.* Ed. Matthew J. Bruccoli. Columbus: Ohio State University Press.

--- (1959). *Literary Publishing in America, 1790-1850.* Philadelphia: University of Pennsylvania Press.

Coultrap-McQuin, Susan (1990). *Doing Literary Business: American Women Writers in the Nineteenth Century*. Chapel Hill: The University of North Carolina Press.

Davidson, Cathy N. (2004). *Revolution and the Word: The Rise of the Novel in America.* Exp. Ed. Oxford: Oxford University Press.

Fern, Fanny [Pseud. Sara Payson Willis Parton] (1986). *Ruth Hall and Other Writings.* Ed. Joyce W. Warren. New Brunswick: Rutgers University Press.

Gilmore, Michael T. (1985). *American Romanticism and the Marketplace*. Chicago: University of Chicago Press.

Glickman, Lawrence B. (1999) "Introduction." *Consumer Society in American History: A Reader*. Ed. L. B. G. Ithaca: Cornell University Press, 1-14.

Hoganson, Kristin (2007). *Consumer's Imperium: The Global Production of American Domesticity, 1865-1920.* Chapel Hill: University of North Carolina Press.

Hunter, James Davidson and Joshua J. Yates (2011). "Introduction: Thrift and Thriving in America." *Thrift and Thriving in America: Capitalism and Moral*

Order from the Puritans to the Present. Eds. J. J. Y. and J. D. H. Oxford: Oxford University Press.

Jackson, Leon (2007). *The Business of Letters: Authorial Economies in Antebellum America.* Berkeley: Stanford University Press.

Jaffee, David (2011). *A New Nation of Goods: Artisans, Consumers, and Commodities in Early America, 1790-1860.* Philadelphia: University of Pennsylvania Press.

Kelley, Mary (1984). *Public Women Private Stage: Literary Domesticity in Nineteenth-Century America.* New York: Oxford University Press.

Kirkland, Caroline (1999 [1838]). *A New Home, Who'll Follow? Or Glimpses of Western Life.* Ed. Sandra A. Zagarell. New Brunswick: Rutgers University Press.

Machor, James L. (2011). *Reading Fiction in Antebellum America: Informed Response and Reception Histories, 1820-1865.* Baltimore: Johns Hopkins University Press.

McCarthy, Kathleen D. (2011). "Spreading the Gospel of Self-Denial: Thrift and Association in Antebellum America." *Thrift and Thriving in America: Capitalism and Moral Order from the Puritans to the Present.* Eds. Joshua J. Yates and James Davidson Hunter. Oxford: Oxford University Press, 160-182.

McGovern, Charles F. (2006). *Sold American: Consumption and Citizenship, 1890-1945.* Chapel Hill: University of North Carolina Press.

Merish, Lori (2000). *Sentimental Materialism: Gender, Commodity Culture, and Nineteenth-Century American Literature.* Durham: Duke University Press.

Michaels, Walter Benn (1987). *The Gold Standard and the Logic of Naturalism: American Literature at the Turn of the Century.* Berkeley: University of California Press.

Robbins, Sarah (2004). *Managing Literacy, Mothering America: Women's Narratives on Reading and Writing in the Nineteenth Century.* Pittsburgh: University of Pittsburgh Press.

Shammas, Carole (1990). *The Pre-industrial Consumer in England and America.* Oxford: Clarendon Press.

Sherman, Sarah Way (2013). *Sacramental Shopping: Louise May Alcott, Edith Wharton, and the Spirit of Modern Consumerism.* New Hampshire: University Press of New England.

---, (2005). "Mapping the Culture of Abundance: Literary Narratives and Consumer Culture." *A Companion to American Fiction 1865-1914.* Eds. Robert Paul Lamb and G.R. Thompson. Malden: Blackwell.

Sigourney, Lydia Huntley (1838). "Letter XIII: Reading and Thinking." *Letters to Mothers.* Hartford: Hudson and Skinner, 145-152.

Teichgraeber III, Richard F. (1995). *Sublime Thoughts/ Penny Wisdom. Situating Emerson and Thoreau in the American Market.* Baltimore: Johns Hopkins University Press.

Thoreau, Henry David (1992 [1854]). *Walden and Resistance to Civil Government.* Ed. William Rossi. NY: Norton.

Tischleder, Babette B. (2014). *The Literary Life of Things: Case Studies in American Fiction.* Frankfurt: Campus.

Warren, Joyce W. (1986). "Introduction." *Ruth Hall and Other Writings.* By Fanny Fern. New Brunswick: Rutgers University Press, ix-xliii.

Zboray, Ronald J. (1989). "Antebellum Reading and the Ironies of Technological Innovation." *Reading in America. Literature & Social History.* Ed. Cathy N. Davidson. Baltimore: The Johns Hopkins University Press, 180-200.

Katja Kanzler (Dresden)

Discourses of Production and Consumption in New England 'Factory Girl' Literature

This article engages with a 'minority' tradition in early nineteenth-century U.S. literature and culture, a literary phenomenon that seems to share with the period's most famous aesthetic movement – transcendentalism – only its roots in a small town in New England: the culture and literature of 'mill' or 'factory girls' in Lowell, Massachusetts.[1] This culture found its outlet in numerous literary magazines published across New England mill towns, magazines often edited by and featuring the writing of female mill workers.[2] The *Lowell Offering* – which appeared, with one intermission, from 1840 to 1845 – was both the most widely known of these magazines and the one with the longest life span. The factory-girl culture from which these magazines originated was similarly short-lived. As Thomas Dublin's pioneering historical research outlines, in the first decades of their existence, New England's textile mills recruited much of their workforce among young women from the region's rural areas. This first generation of female mill workers – daughters of yeomen farmers – tended to understand their sojourn at the factory as temporary, typically geared toward saving some money before they would get married. They brought with them not only a Calvinist work ethic, which sustained them through brutally long workdays, but also an interest in 'self-improvement' through attending lectures and participating in 'Self-Improvement Circles' after work. Out of one such circle, the project of the *Lowell Offering* developed, a magazine that assembled various types of writing – sketches, tales, essays, poetry –, all written by women employed at one of Lowell's factories.[3]

Today, the literary culture borne by the town of Lowell in the eighteen-forties looks back on several decades of either scholarly neglect or condescension. As many other forms of 'minority' literature, it had long been the primary province of historians interested in the historical dynamics it documents rather than in its textuality. When literary scholars dealt with the *Lowell Offering*, they often found it lacking in aesthetic as well as political merit. In one of the first studies dedicated to working women's literary magazines, Bertha Stearns calls the *Lowell Offering*

> pathetically imitative of the ladies' magazines with which the period was so lavishly supplied. It offered its readers naïve stories of happy love, brief essays on moral and religious topics, descriptions of American scenes, occasional biographical sketches, letters, literary reviews, and comments on contemporary writers, just as periodicals addressed to women always had.[4]

In a more recent study Kristie Hamilton argues that "the *Offering* sketches' adherence to bourgeois literary paradigms and bourgeois 'femininity' constituted an evasion of worker interests because it idealized uncomplaining passivity."[5] The disappointment with the *Lowell Offering* that both scholars express originates in their sense of its texts as 'imitative' – as merely copying the literary formats, styles, and cultural values of the middle-class women whom the period's hegemonic gender discourse posits as metonymic representatives of 'true womanhood.'[6] Self-evidently expecting working women's literature to pursue a political project – to represent "worker interests"[7] – they find it lacking in politics, or showcasing the wrong politics by allowing itself to be co-opted by the interests of capital.

My approach to antebellum factory-girl literature situates itself within a recent shift in scholarship that challenges and amends such one-dimensionally critical readings by trying to come to terms with this literature's own, 'minoritarian' dynamics.[8] I think of the *Lowell Offering*'s use of bourgeois ideas and conventions not as passive imitation, but as active appropriation, efforts made by writers marginalized by overlapping systems of gender and class to forge an affirmative subject position and write themselves into American culture. This effort is conflicted and precarious: qualities surfacing in the short life spans of magazines dedicated to this literature, or in this literature's re-appropriation by stakeholders in Lowell's companies, who would use its narratives to de-legitimize and silence protests against working conditions in their factories.

In the following, I am interested in the ways in which this precariousness registers in the texts themselves. I will explore telling moments of evasion or lapses that betray the hard discursive work performed in these texts – the work of using well-established conventions and discourses to articulate and celebrate a subject position that these very discourses were in the process of 'othering' and marginalizing.

The particular discourse on which I focus is that of consumption. As I will outline, many of the *Lowell Offering*'s texts employ a discourse of consumption to authorize the multiply marginalized subject position of the factory girl and to assert her cultural equality with middle-class women. This recurrent reliance on a discourse of consumption is, of course, highly paradoxical in a literary project whose authors and protagonists identify as 'factory girls' – i.e., in terms of their position in processes of production. In fact, scenes of industrial production play a notably marginal role in the texts. I will explore the paradoxical presence of consumption and near-absence of production in the narratives of the *Lowell Offering* as an instance of the precarious appropriation outlined above, a moment where the magazine's texts endeavor to use and adapt a sanctioned discourse of feminine personhood and agency.

1. Consumption and Feminine Selfhood in Antebellum America

I preface my readings by sketching – in very broad strokes – the socio-cultural context that turns consumption into an affirmative language of (middle-class) feminine selfhood in the first half of the nineteenth century. Several social and cultural historians have described how, in this period, an "increasing salience of class"[9] goes hand in hand with significant changes in hegemonic conceptions of work, leisure, and consumption. As Stuart Blumin outlines in his magisterial study of American class formations, the Jacksonian era sees the emergence of both a discernible middle class and of a self-conscious working class. Transformations in the discourse of work play a key role in the simultaneous and interdependent developments of middle and working classes. The notion of work splits into 'manual' and 'non-manual,' and the distinction between them underwrites much of the emerging discourse of social distinction.[10] This bifurcated concept of work also lies at the heart of Bromell's exploration of literary representations of labor in this period. He argues that "the distinction between mental and manual labor, resting upon an assumed dichotomy of mind and matter, was the paradigm that structured virtually all antebellum thinking about work."[11] As Bromell demonstrates, the discursive alignment of this bifurcated notion of work with the Cartesian duality of mind and body shapes the value attached to these two forms of work and their semantic contribution to conceptions of social distinction.

Along with the socio-cultural de-valorization of manual labor, this new value placed upon non-manual forms of work markedly intervenes in the ethos of simplicity that David Shi discusses as a foundational component of U.S. American culture. Prior to the nineteenth century, the republican thought that governed public discourse in the age of the Revolution and the Early Republic valued work – the visible performance of manual labor – as both catalyst and evidence of virtuousness. 'Industry' figured centrally among the cardinal virtues of republicanism, next to "frugality, simplicity, enlightened thinking, and public spiritedness."[12] The first half of the nineteenth century bears witness to an erosion of this republican ethos of simplicity, Shi notes, "giv[ing] way to an expansive commercial and urban outlook promoting economic individualism, social mobility, political equality, and material gratification."[13] In the course of this process, white-collar labor and non-manual activities associated with leisure rather than work become key touchstones of 'good' selfhood – intellectual and affective activities understood to cultivate the individual's mind and soul.[14]

This recoding of time spent without physical labor from 'idleness' to 'leisure' – from a non-productivity detrimental to the individual as well as the community to time 'free from toil' that could be used to develop the 'faculties of the mind and soul' – is as intricately intertwined with class formation as the new valorization of non-manual work. There is another cultural practice and discourse that is deeply connected with the social transformations Blumin describes: the discourse and practice of consumption. Consumption in general, particularly discourses and practices associated with the furnishing of the home begin to figure as key emblems of middle-class identity. Interrogating early nineteenth-century discourses of consumption, Lori Merish highlights the central role that domesticity plays: "Middle-class consumption was produced in tandem with the new ideal of domestic womanhood,"[15] she argues, adding that "the domestication of display and politeness, and the consumption of goods that give shape to these practices, incorporates aristocratic categories of civility and politeness into a distinctly middle-class domestic ethic."[16]

According to Merish, then, performances of consumption exhibit both middle-class status and 'true womanhood.' Coalescing in the overdetermined space of the private home, emerging notions of refinement and feminine virtue considerably depend on one another. The domestic woman who conspicuously abstains from salaried or waged labor and whose 'work' primarily rests in acts of 'tasteful' consumption becomes a status symbol.[17] At the same time, the newly valued practice of domestic consumption offers (middle-class) women a discursive foil that authorized their agency and participation in the public sphere, if on severely limited terms. Merish locates this empowering potential in the rise of a "new cultural type of feminine civil subjectivity" that she dubs "the republican consumer." She notes that by "[e]ndowing feminine taste and emotional preference with 'civilizing' efficacy, early republican texts legitimized women's participation in the market as consumers and thus defined a new civic identification for women as liberal subjects."[18]

It is this new valorization of consumption in early nineteenth-century culture, and its resonance with hegemonic notions of femininity, that makes the discourse useful for factory-girl writers in their effort to carve out an affirmative subject position. It offers them a sanctioned language to articulate the independence specific to their situation – making money all their own, and living free from supervision by either fathers or husbands – and to do so within affirmative narratives of feminine selfhood and agency.[19] But the discourse of consumption proves ambivalent for the literary project of Lowell's factory girls. While they could exploit its alignment with gender, its association with class proved problematic for them. Consumption ascended to a culturally valued practice in the course of its instrumentalization for middle-class distinction – distinction, that is, from a working class which, of course, included industrial workers. As Gerda Lerner's pioneering study of social stratification among early nineteenth-century women suggests, the 'lady' and the 'mill girl' stand for the opposing ends in an American society increasingly thought of as divided along lines of class. Consumption evolved as a key idiom for articulating the difference between them. Despite careful efforts to adapt and translate the discourse of consumption for narratives of the factory girl, this ambivalence surfaces in the texts of the *Lowell Offering*.

2. Scenes of Production and Consumption in the *Lowell Offering*

The maneuvers by which the texts of the *Lowell Offering* seek to appropriate these dominant discursive formations register, first of all, in their avoidance or transfiguration of scenes of industrial production. This avoidance is conspicuous and telling in a literary project that defines itself as a magazine by and about factory girls. Most notably, factories do not constitute the main setting in the texts of the *Lowell Offering*. It is rather the boardinghouse to which texts tend to direct their attention, constructing it as a domestic space in which the company of fellow workers provides their protagonists with surrogate families. Sketches like "Home in a Boarding-House" or "Our Household"[20] use the private home that so many contemporary texts elaborate as a touchstone to present the unfamiliar space of a boardinghouse to non-factory readers. By this strategy, the texts not only counter the pervasive imaging of the factory boardinghouse as a thinly disguised brothel in popular sensationalist literature.[21] They are also able to stage the factory girl in familiar performances of femininity – building and maintaining relationships with members of their surrogate families, writing letters home, reading, and shopping. These activities I will discuss in greater detail below. The preference for the boardinghouse and its depiction as home pave the ground for many of the magazine's strategies of appropriation, its adaptation of elements and conventions of middle-class women's domestic literature.

When texts turn their attention to the factory, they frequently do so in narratives organized around the topos of the guided tour. As Sylvia Jenkins Cook and others have noted, the town of Lowell and the model of industrial labor realized there evolved into a veritable tourist attraction in the eighteen-thirties and –forties.[22] Several of its visitors wrote about their tourist experiences in texts that greatly influenced the public image of Lowell – visitors such as Charles Dickens, Anthony Trollope, or Frederika Bremer. Many texts in the *Lowell Offering* adopt this convention and take their readers on virtual tours of the town. In the process, they frame the factory as an object of tourist consumption, rather than as a place of labor and production. The sketch "A Second Peep at Factory Life" is exemplary here. Its first-person narrator – a factory-girl character – directly addresses the reader as a "dear friend" whom she invites to "do as the factory girls do."[23] Yet contrary to this promise of an 'authentic' narrative of the factory-girl experience, the text delivers a tourist experience: Its narrator takes the reader on a tour of the town, guiding her or him through the various rooms of a textile mill, through the streets to a boardinghouse. In the process, the narrative presents the buildings of the mill town, their exteriors and interiors, as aesthetic spectacles. The moment in which the text presents the first glimpse of a factory is telling:

> we will stop on the slight elevation by the gate, and view the mills. The one to the left rears high its huge sides of brick and mortar, and the belfry, towering far above the rest, stands out in bold relief against the rosy sky. The almost innumerable windows glitter, like gems, in the morning sunlight. It is six and a half stories high, and, like the fabled monster of old, who guarded the sacred waters of Mars, it seems to guard its less aspiring sister to the right [...]. ("Peep" 77)

In accordance with the script of a guided tour, it is first the exterior of the factory building to which the text attends. The passage frames the factory building in a way that notably aestheticizes and romanticizes it. It encodes a gaze at industrial scenery from a vantage point of distance, a distance that enables the aesthetic effects and romantic similes that govern the description.

Eventually, the narrator does enter the factory, yet – in keeping with her role – not as a worker but as a tour guide. The aesthetic gaze that actualizes the text's commodification of the mill town as a tourist attraction also controls its depiction of industrial production inside the factory:

> Here we have spinning jacks or jennies that dance merrily along whizzing and singing, as they spin out their 'long yarns,' and it seems but pleasure to watch their movements; but it is hard work, and requires good health and much strength. ("Peep" 78)

Interestingly, in the short final clause of this passage ("but it is hard work, and requires good health and much strength"), a different perspective surfaces, one that shifts the attention from watching the machines to working them, from framing them as aesthetic spectacle to a scene of industrial labor. This is a fleeting moment that the text, symptomatically, does not develop, a moment in which the factory girl – as the subject who performs the "hard work" – does not figure at all.

"A Second Peep of Factory Life" is exemplary in its reluctance to represent the factory as a space of industrial production and, in particular, to depict the factory girl as a worker.[24] This palpable evasion is set off by the numerous instances in which the *Lowell Offering*'s texts stage the factory girl as a consumer. Again and again, scenes of consumption allow the factory girl to engage in well-established performances of womanhood. They are also key textual instances in which she is cast as an agent and subject. I would like to explore this dynamic in two texts.[25] The first one bears the indicative title "Leisure Hours of the Mill Girls." It is exemplary of several sketches published in the magazine that employ a didactic mode, featuring an authorial narrator who juxtaposes 'right' and 'wrong' models of factory-girl behavior. The text begins with the pedagogical question "The leisure hours of the Mill girls – how shall they be spent?"[26] and proceeds by having a group of women represent different ways in which factory girls would use their time off from work. Indicatively, much of the leisure activities that the sketch discusses involve consumer practices. First they are invoked to develop the character of Charlotte as the most blatant model of 'wrong' behavior. Charlotte's weakness in character expresses itself in her vulnerability to the temptations of Lowell's consumer infrastructure. Lacking in proper self-control, she spends both her time and her money consuming goods. These – fashion and candy – connote an indulgence in desire and appetite rather than the satisfaction of needs, while her family members lack life's most basic necessities:

> her folks had been known to jump for joy at the sight of a crust of bread. She spends every cent of her wages for dress and confectionary. She has gone out now; and she will come back with lemons, sugar, rich cake, and so on. ("Leisure" 99)

A second character, Bertha, is established as a morally more ambiguous character, again by highlighting her consumer behavior. Her conduct appears more responsible, but only at first sight:

> I buy three volumes of novels every month; and when that is not enough, I take some from the circulating library. I think it is our duty to improve our minds as much as possible, now the Mill girls are beginning to be thought so much of. ("Leisure" 99)

Bertha's consumer practices seem to signify her internalization of the value and importance of self-improvement. But the way in which she organizes her education reflects that she has not fully learned the lessons on self-improvement: She consumes the wrong kind of literature, indiscriminately and too much of it. Bertha embodies an undisciplined and hedonistic mode of leisure behavior that echoes Charlotte's, excessively indulging in the consumption of goods marked as unnecessary luxuries that are 'bad' for her.

While both Charlotte and Bertha thus represent the wrongs of unregulated and excessive consumption, other characters dramatize the flaws of a complete refusal to engage in consumer activities. One of them, Ann, simply finds nothing to do in her time off from work, an inactivity that the narrator describes as 'idleness' ("Leisure" 99). Two other characters, the Clark sisters, spend their spare time working, making dresses and cloth to augment their income. Interestingly, the narrative does not frame the scene of the busily working sisters as 'industry,' as a laudable expression of their work ethic, but as another 'wrong' choice of leisure activities – wrong because it prioritizes making money over self-improvement. The narrator eventually reflects on the women's conduct:

> The Clark girls do not, as yet, coalesce in their system of improvement. They still prefer making netting and dresses, to the lecture room, the improvement circle, and even to the reading of the 'Book of books.' So difficult is it to turn from the worship of Plutus! ("Leisure" 112)

The text closes with such narratorial reflections on all the protagonists. Ann, Charlotte, and Bertha are presented as reformed characters. Their awakening to and reform of their flaws provide the kind of role models that didactic narratives typically elaborate. Ann, the narrator notes in a brief comment, "is now an excellent lady" ("Leisure" 112) who seems to have finally learned the importance of self-improvement. The other two characters receive more attention:

> The delusion of Bertha and Charlotte is partially broken. – Bertha is beginning to understand that much reading does not naturally result in intellectual or moral improvement, unless it be well regulated. Charlotte is learning that 'to enjoy is to obey;' and that to pamper her own animal appetites, while her father and mother are suffering for want of the necessities of life, is not in obedience to Divine command ("Leisure" 112)

Overall, the text's obvious concern with the ways in which workers spend their few hours off from work, along with its didactic orientation, invites a reading as an effort to discipline working women – women who live removed from both parental control and supervision by middle-class philanthropists. However, I aim to highlight another dimension of the text. Its preoccupation with 'proper' and 'improper' ways in which factory girls spend their leisure time can also be read as a strategy for casting working women as virtuous subjects. It imagines factory girls as agents by focusing on the choices they make in deciding what to do with their money and how to organize their spare time. The particular activities that the text champions with didactic clarity reflect the values encoded in the period's dominant discourses of leisure and consumption that I have outlined above, the values of self-improvement and a sense of civic (in this case, familial) responsibility. Taking my cue from Merish, I see the text not necessarily disciplining working women as much as staging them in well-established scenes of feminine agency, as virtuous republican consumers. In this period's literature, female characters are typically allowed to make only two kinds of choices – whom to marry and what to buy. In fact, the text's adaptation of the latter blueprint for feminine agency reflects how such narratives of women's consumer choices are modeled on the more traditional narratives of women's spousal choices. The conventions of the seduction novel shine through in the juxtaposition of 'irresponsible' impulsiveness and indulgence in 'libidinal' desires with 'responsible' self-restraint and parental obedience. The didactic concern with 'right' and 'wrong' makes the characters' consumer choices 'matter.' It endows them with both moral and social significance. Performances of responsible consumption and leisure activities are claimed as exhibiting a particularly feminine brand of civic virtue.[27]

A similar dynamic can be traced in the sketch "Evening Before Pay-Day." As its title indicates, the text casts money as the central aspect of the factory experience by observing a group of factory girls who are looking forward to the day when they receive their wages as the most significant one of the week. Even more insistently than "Leisure Hours of the Mill Girls," the sketch thus depicts the agency that employed labor facilitates for factory girls as revolving around consumer choices. This text, too, features a variety of voices that represent ways of spending which are framed as more or less appropriate. One character attracts criticism for "spend[ing] almost all [her] money in dress."[28] Another one gets chided for her stinginess ("Evening" 163) and a third for worshipping her savings account ("Sundays she stays here reckoning up her interest, while we are at meeting," "Evening" 165). The second part of the text focuses on Rosina, one of the characters criticized for her excessive economy, who wears a dress "so shabby," another character nags her, "I should not wonder if it should soon drop off your back" ("Evening" 165). The text eventually reveals that Rosina's efforts to save money are not driven by stinginess, but by her dedication to supporting a widowed mother and an infirm sister.

In accordance with dominant discourses of sentimental femininity, the narrative applauds Rosina's self-denial in the service of the weak and suffering. Yet next to Rosina's heroic selflessness, it points to another character as a perhaps more tangible role model – Lucy, who announces to use her wages to buy "a pretty new, though cheap, bonnet, and I shall also pay my quarter's pew-rent, and a year's subscription to the Lowell Offering" as well as to "lay aside half of every month's wages" ("Evening" 166). Lucy stands for a balanced way of spending that contrasts with the excessiveness of the other characters. The virtuousness that her consumer habits exhibit rests not in selflessness, but in moderation, and in the sensible deliberation of every consumer decision. Lucy's sense and self-discipline, dramatized in the context of consumer practices, make her the model of a feminine virtue that does not define itself in terms of self-denial, but in terms of an agency grounded in civic responsibility.

Both texts, "Leisure Hours of the Mill Girls" and "Evening Before Pay-Day," thus use a discourse of consumption to articulate the factory girl's independence and agency, and to construct these as virtuous and co-extensive with sanctioned (i.e., middle-class) models of femininity. In addition, they cast the consumer market as a site of democratization, where the factory girl finds herself enfranchised thanks to the money she earns by her labor and where she can procure the self-improvement and refinement that bear a promise of upward mobility.

But the marketplace and the discourse of consumption attached to it also figure as frameworks in which the texts reflect on the limitations of the factory girl's agency and of the franchise she may enjoy. This dimension surfaces, for example, when a character in "Evening Before Pay-Day" notes: "we cannot procure a year's seat in one of our most expensive churches for less than your present week's wages" ("Evening" 164); or when the Clark sisters in "Leisure Hours of the Mill Girls" explain why they spend their spare time working rather than reading: "'I don't make but twelve dollars a month [...]. We can't afford to [read]" ("Leisure" 102). In these passages, the texts contemplate how the consumer culture they celebrate elsewhere as a force of democratization also draws lines of exclusion, lines acutely felt by Lowell's workers due to their meager wages. Pointing to the factory girls' meager wages, the texts, after all, do consider these women's position in contexts of production, in New England's early industrial economy. In so doing, they acknowledge – however fleetingly – the forces of economic stratification and social distinction that permeate an industrializing American society, forces that increasingly position industrial workers as the 'others' against which the middle class defines itself.

Notes

[1] Let me highlight at this point that I use the terms 'mill girl' and 'factory girl' to designate the cultural figure and identification articulated in early nineteenth-century texts, rather than the actual women who worked at the cotton mills in Lowell. Concerning the comparison between Lowell and Concord, see Cook (2008) for a fuller development (39-41).

[2] Judith Ranta's (1999) excellent *Annotated Guide to Nineteenth-Century American Textile Factory Literature* provides an overview of the factory-girl magazines published in New England, some of which ran for only a few months. The archive of factory-girl literature that Ranta researched is quite substantial. She notes: "[o]f the 457 texts annotated in this volume, some thirty-six percent [...] were probably or definitely written by mill workers" (ix).

[3] Thomas Dublin's (1979) *Women at Work* still provides the most comprehensive historical study of Lowell's female industrial workforce in the early nineteenth century. For a discussion of the history of the *Lowell Offering*, see Foner (1977), 26-29; Eisler (1998), 33-41; and Stearns (1930).

[4] Bertha Monica Stearns (1930). "Early Factory Magazines in New England." *Journal of Economic and Business History* 2.4, 690-691 (685-705).

[5] Kristie Hamilton (1998). *America's Sketchbook: The Cultural Life of a Nineteenth-Century Literary Genre.* Athens: Ohio University Press, 112. As several other scholars, Hamilton contrasts the *Lowell Offering* with labor-activist publications like the *Voice of Industry*, whose texts openly contested the *Offering*'s depictions of industrial labor and decried the working conditions at Lowell's factories. The two magazines reflect the extent to which the poetics and politics of representing work and industrialism were the subject of heated debates in the first half of the nineteenth century. For a discussion of the factory girl as a "contested sign" (xvii) in this debate, see Amireh (2000), 1-40.

[6] 'True womanhood,' of course, invokes Barbara Welter's (1966) classic study of the antebellum period's hegemonic discourse of femininity as revolving around ideals of piety, purity, domesticity, and submissiveness.

[7] Hamilton (1998), 112.

[8] A key example of scholarship that engages with the minoritarian dynamics of factory-girl literature is Mary Loeffelholz's study of Lucy Larcom's poetry, where she argues that "[t]he central topic of Larcom's [writing] is not primarily the material conditions of the millworkers' industrial labor [...]. Her theme is, rather, the mill girls' access to culture and the role of culture in the making of class" (6). See also Freeman (1994), Cady (2012), Merish (2012, "Factory").
[9] Stuart M. Blumin (1989). *The Emergence of the Middle Class: Social Experience in the American City, 1760-1900*. Cambridge: Cambridge University Press, 66.
[10] *Ibid.*, 66-68.
[11] Nicholas K. Bromell (1993). *By the Sweat of the Brow: Literature and Labor in Antebellum America*. Chicago: University of Chicago Press, 10-11.
[12] David Shi (1985). *The Simple Life: Plain Living and High Thinking in American Culture*. Athens: University of Georgia Press, 52.
[13] *Ibid.*, 100.
[14] One of the examples by which Shi illustrates this shift is the utopian experiment of Brook Farm: "Its residents were determined, as one of them wrote, 'to secure as many hours as possible from necessary toil' in order to spend more leisure time 'for the production of intellectual goods' [...]. Brook Farm, one visitor wrote, 'aims to be rich, not in the metallic representation of wealth, but in wealth itself, which money should represent, namely, *leisure to live in all the faculties of the soul*'" (134; emphasis in the text).
[15] Lori Merish (2000). *Sentimental Materialism: Gender, Commodity Culture, and Nineteenth-Century American Literature*. Durham: Duke University Press, 2.
[16] *Ibid.*, 68.
[17] Cf. Gerda Lerner (1979). "The Lady and the Mill Girl: Changes in the Status of Women in the Age of Jackson." *A Heritage of Her Own: Toward a New Social History of American Women*. Eds. Nancy F. Cott and Elizabeth Hafkin Pleck. New York: Simon & Schuster, 7-15. Rpt. from *American Studies Journal* 10.1 (1969), 5-15. Here: cf. 12 (7-15).
[18] Merish (2000), 18.
[19] In doing so, these factory-girl writers confronted a literary tradition of narrativizing female independence as vulnerability to 'seduction' – the 'unprotected' young woman is a stock figure of the seduction novel. At the same time as the *Lowell Offering* and similar magazines tried to develop affirmative narratives of the factory girl, sensationalist literature also began to use her as a character. For a discussion of sensationalist narratives of the factory girl, see Amireh (2000), 30-33; and Merish (2012, "Factory").
[20] Most pieces of factory-girl literature have been published anonymously or under pseudonyms. I therefore cite my primary texts by their titles. In the bibliography, I give the name of the author as she signed her text; in brackets, I indicate, the person to whom the pseudonym or initials have been traced by Benita Eisler.

[21] The novel *Mary Bean: The Factory Girl*, for example, is quite explicit in analogizing the factory boardinghouse with a brothel. Its female protagonist elopes to a mill town, where the novel's villain 'seduces' her on the first night she spends in a boardinghouse. He then visits and leaves her at will, taking full advantage of the freedom from commitment enabled by such living arrangements. As Paul Erickson (2005) notes in his study of antebellum sensationalist fiction, this literature generally delights in uncovering an infrastructure of prostitution behind urban facades, and the overwhelmingly female population in mill towns particularly inspired the sensationalist imagination.
[22] Sylvia Jenkins Cook (2008). *Working Women, Literary Ladies: The Industrial Revolution and Female Aspiration*. Oxford: Oxford University Press, 43.
[23] J. L. B. [Josephine L. Baker] (1845). "A Second Peep at Factory Life." *The Lowell Offering* 5. Rpt. in: Eisler, Benita (ed.) (1998). *The Lowell Offering: Writings by New England Mill Women (1840-1845)*. New York: Norton, 77 (77-82). Further references to this edition will be included in the text. References in the text use a shortened form of the story's title.
[24] Merish explores how contemporary labor-activist writing specifically addresses and criticizes this evasion of industrial production in factory-girl literature, reading these as moments where working-class writers reflect on the limitations placed upon their literary projects by dominant conceptions of literary aesthetics: "The author [of one such critical text] presents a pointed critique of how 'taste' at once produced and gratified by literary discourse, places working-class material 'reality' [...] beyond literary representation" ("Factory" 15).
[25] For a reading that interrogates how the two texts I will discuss below use a discourse of money for tropes of personhood, see my "'Pay Day'" (2012).
[26] D. [Eliza J. Cate] (1842). "Leisure Hours of the Mill Girls." *The Lowell Offering* 2. Rpt. in: Eisler (1998), 99 (99-112). Further references to this edition will be included in the text. References in the text use a shortened form of the story's title.
[27] Looking at representations of consumption in factory-girl literature from another perspective, to Merish these texts challenge hegemonic conceptions of feminine desire as bound to domesticity, and as culminating in acts of self-sacrifice by highlighting "forms of workingwomen's desire – consumer desire, sexual desire, the pleasures of urban leisure culture, the affective intensities and homoerotics of the female peer culture of boardinghouse and workplace, the prospect of female economic and social 'ambition' – associated with independent wage earning and the novel pleasures of working-class urban life" ("Factory" 5).
[28] Lucinda [Harriet Farley] (1841). "Evening Before Pay-Day." *The Lowell Offering* 1. Rpt. in: Eisler (1998), 164 (162-172). Further references to this edition will be included in the text. References use a shortened form of the story's title.

Bibliography

Amireh, Amal (2000). *The Factory Girl and the Seamstress: Imagining Gender and Class in Nineteenth-Century American Fiction.* New York: Garland.

Anon. (1842). "Home in a Boarding-House." *The Lowell Offering* 3. Rpt. in: Eisler, Benita (ed.) (1998). *The Lowell Offering: Writings by New England Mill Women (1840-1845).* New York: Norton, 73.

Blumin, Stuart M. (1989). *The Emergence of the Middle Class: Social Experience in the American City, 1760-1900.* Cambridge: Cambridge University Press.

Bromell, Nicholas K. (1993). *By the Sweat of the Brow: Literature and Labor in Antebellum America.* Chicago: University of Chicago Press.

Cady, Kathryn A. (2012). "'Ann and Myself': Rhetoric, Sexualities, and Silence at Lowell." *Southern Communication Journal* 77.1, 24-44.

Cook, Sylvia Jenkins (2008). *Working Women, Literary Ladies: The Industrial Revolution and Female Aspiration.* Oxford: Oxford University Press.

D. [Eliza J. Cate] (1842)."Leisure Hours of the Mill Girls." *The Lowell Offering* 2. Rpt. in: Eisler, Benita (ed.) (1998). *The Lowell Offering: Writings by New England Mill Women (1840-1845).* New York: Norton, 99-112.

Dublin, Thomas (1979). *Women at Work: The Transformation of Work and Community in Lowell, Massachusetts, 1826-1860.* New York: Columbia University Press.

Eisler, Benita (ed.) (1998). *The Lowell Offering: Writings by New England Mill Women (1840-1845).* New York: Norton.

Erickson, Paul Joseph (2005). "Welcome to Sodom: The Cultural Work of City-Mysteries Fiction in Antebellum America." Dissertational Thesis. University of Texas, Austin.

Foner, Philip S. (ed.) (1977). *The Factory Girls: A Collection of Writings on Life and Struggles in the New England Factories of the 1840s by the Factory Girls Themselves and the Story, in Their Own Words, of the First Trade Unions of Women Workers in the United States.* Urbana: University of Illinois Press.

Freeman, Elizabeth (1994). "'What Factory Girls Had Power to Do': The Techno-Logic of Working-Class Feminine Publicity in *The Lowell Offering." Arizona Quarterly* 50.2, 109-128.

Hamilton, Kristie (1998). *America's Sketchbook: The Cultural Life of a Nineteenth-Century Literary Genre.* Athens: Ohio University Press.

H. T. (1841). "Our Household." *The Lowell Offering* 1.12, 364-365.

J. A. B. (1850). Mary Bean: *The Factory Girl. A Domestic Story, Illustrative of the Trials and Temptations of Factory Life. Founded on Recent Events.* Hotchkiss: Boston.

J. L. B. [Josephine L. Baker] (1845)."A Second Peep at Factory Life." *The Lowell Offering* 5. Rpt. in: Eisler, Benita (ed.) (1998). *The Lowell Offering: Writings by New England Mill Women (1840-1845).* New York: Norton, 77-82.

Kanzler, Katja (2012). "'Pay Day': Discourses of Money in Literature by Antebellum 'Factory Girls.'" *American Economies.* Ed. Eva Boesenberg, Reinhard Isensee, and Martin Klepper. Heidelberg: Winter, 349-364.

Lerner, Gerda (1979). "The Lady and the Mill Girl: Changes in the Status of Women in the Age of Jackson." *A Heritage of Her Own: Toward a New Social History of American Women.* Eds. Nancy F. Cott and Elizabeth Hafkin Pleck. New York: Simon & Schuster, 7-15. Rpt. from *American Studies Journal* 10.1 (1969), 5-15.

Loeffelholz, Mary (2007). "'A Strange Medley-Book': Lucy Larcom's *An Idyll of Work.*" *The New England Quarterly* 80.1, 5-34.

Lucinda [Harriet Farley] (1841). "Evening Before Pay-Day." *The Lowell Offering* 1. Rpt. in: Eisler, Benita (ed.) (1998). *The Lowell Offering: Writings by New England Mill Women (1840-1845).* New York: Norton, 162-172.

Merish, Lori (2012). "Factory Labor and Literary Aesthetics: The 'Lowell Mill Girl,' Popular Fiction, and the Proletarian Grotesque." *Arizona Quarterly* 68.4, 1-34.

--- (2000). *Sentimental Materialism: Gender, Commodity Culture, and Nineteenth-Century American Literature.* Durham: Duke University Press.

Ranta, Judith A. (1999). *Women and Children of the Mills: An Annotated Guide to Nineteenth-Century American Textile Factory Literature.* Westport: Greenwood.

Shi, David (1985). *The Simple Life: Plain Living and High Thinking in American Culture.* Athens: University of Georgia Press.

Stearns, Bertha Monica (1930). "Early Factory Magazines in New England." *Journal of Economic and Business History* 2.4, 685-705.

Welter, Barbara (1966). "The Cult of True Womanhood: 1820-1860." *American Quarterly* 18.1, 151-174.

Nicole Maruo-Schröder (Koblenz-Landau)

A "Dish Offered to the Public": The Business of Gender and Class in Nathaniel Hawthorne's *The House of the Seven Gables*

The first half of the nineteenth century saw a number of significant changes in America's cultural, social, and economic structures, many of which were interrelated. At roughly the same time that the young nation developed a sense of a truly original, 'self-made' American literature, this literature became a mass commodity, turning its authors into professionals who had to sell their wares in an increasingly competitive literary marketplace. While this provided new opportunities for many writers – particularly women – who could now profitably earn money with their pens, it also transformed artists into 'mere' professionals, who had to align their art with the taste of their potential audiences. Their writing was not simply judged in terms of artistic standards. Popularity and financial profit mattered more and more. Such changes were part of a larger development during which the nation's economy shifted from a predominantly production-oriented and in many ways self-subsistent agrarian economy to an industry-based capitalist one that increasingly focused on consumption.[1]

Not only did the nation's economy change profoundly; its social structures were also deeply affected. The new economic opportunities helped to establish a middle class that became progressively more powerful and influential throughout the century. This was, moreover, a class that could, and would, indulge in consumption and thus helped align the economic re-structuring with a social and cultural one. Americans turned away from the ideology of a simple life, a Puritan world view that shunned consumption as a distraction from Christian norms and values. They began to appreciate consumer goods and practices. As Stuart Blumin, Richard Bushman and others have shown, consumption came to replace an older ideology of the simple life. Certain goods and activities that only money could buy came to signify middle-class respectability and propriety.[2]

It is in this context that I will take a closer look at Nathaniel Hawthorne's *The House of the Seven Gables* (1851). Focusing especially on the eponymous house, I will argue that the cent shop inside of it functions as one of the central metaphors with which Hawthorne negotiates the changes – especially with regard to gender and class relations –, which the rapid development of the capitalist marketplace brought to the U.S. in the first half of the nineteenth century. As I will show, the two female characters connected to the house as well as to the cent shop, Hepzibah and Phoebe Pyncheon, are particularly important in this context. Both women work as mirror images of each other, representing different classes and also different ways of dealing with the changed economic realities in the novel. However, Hepzibah and Phoebe cannot only be read as representatives of the upper and middle class respectively and their relations to the changing economic structures. They also embody the new and changing roles that writers and their audiences had at that time and reflect the question whose values and preferences exactly come to dominate the (literary) marketplace. Thus, they can also be interpreted as expressions of Hawthorne's own anxieties regarding the altered circumstances of his profession and artistic calling as a writer. Hence, my essay is organized into four different parts: while the first and the last one build this essay's frame, looking at the beginning and the ending of the novel and the roles that the house(s) and cent shop play, the second and third parts discuss the two female characters and how they can be read both as images for the economic changes and as embodiments of the changing roles of authors and readers in the nineteenth-century literary marketplace.

1. Moving In: The House of the Seven Gables

The narrator of *The House of the Seven Gables* opens the novel's first chapter with a detailed description of the eponymous mansion and the way it was built. Having once been the impressive home of the Pyncheon family, an adequate statement of their wealth and influence, it is now decrepit and run-down. Both the street, which "has long ceased to be a fashionable quarter of the town," and the garden, which is overgrown by moss and weed, reflect this decay.[3] The house itself has the features of a "human countenance," showing "the traces not merely of outward storm and sunshine, but expressive also of the long lapse of mortal life, and accompanying vicissitudes, that have passed within" (5). Having participated so closely in the lives of its inhabitants, it has almost "a life of its own" (22). Its "meditative look," finally, suggests that "it had secrets to keep" (22).

Albeit not quite as sinister as Edgar Allan Poe's House of Usher, of which it is reminiscent, the House of the Seven Gables is introduced as an old mansion which lends itself to both gothic and romantic readings, an impression that is reinforced by the allusions to various ghosts that haunt the old house.[4] This is underscored by the novel's "Preface," in which the narrator famously insists that he is narrating a romance rather than a novel, focusing not so much on the "probable and ordinary course of man's experience" than on the "[m]arvellous," a past "[l]egend," for which he claims "a certain latitude" instead of presenting a mimetic representation of real life (3).

However, almost immediately (at the end of the first chapter) the narrator seems to revoke this impression of the uncanny, the gothic, and the romantic in the character of the house:

> There is one other feature, very essential to be noticed, but which, we greatly fear, may damage *any picturesque and romantic impression*, which we have been willing to throw over our sketch of this respectable edifice. In the front gable, under the impending brow of the second story, and contiguous to the street, was a *shop-door* [...]. (22, my emphasis)

The world of business intrudes unceremoniously into the world of romance, destroying its picturesque and quaint character and, one might add, grounding it in nineteenth-century reality. Far from being a dark romantic secret, the narrator goes on to emphasize, the shop door is a "matter disagreeably delicate to handle," as it reveals plainly and embarrassingly the financial difficulties of "the present occupant of the august Pyncheon-house" (23).

The shop door thus becomes a point of transition both within the story as well as on a metafictional level. On the one hand, it allows the mundane world of money-making, of business, production and consumption, to enter the world of romance, of literature in general, indicating Hawthorne's well-known anxiety with regard to the necessity to earn a living with his pen. Just as the shop door destroys any picturesque and romantic image one might have of *The House of the Seven Gables*, both the house and the romance, the turning of literature into a wholesale commodity destroys not only any romanticized notion one might have of being a writer. It also endangers the 'profession' of the artist (which used to be more of a vocation), making it dependent on the taste of the masses rather than any non-commercial standards of art. Once literature becomes a mass commodity, and it was quickly becoming one during the first decades of the nineteenth century, the writer is in danger of turning from an artist into a huckster, who might have to compromise his or her art for the sake of marketability.[5] Moreover, the writer has to enter the arena of competition, forced to be successful in order to make a living. That this was a danger keenly felt by Hawthorne is well known and most obvious in his infamous comment on "the d——d mob of scribbling women."[6]

And yet, the shop door in the Pyncheon mansion not only constitutes a metaphorical entranceway through which the marketplace enters the literary world (and vice versa). Situating the cent shop inside the aristocratic Pyncheon mansion can also be read as a comment on how the new economic structures affected society, particularly class relations in antebellum America. In other words, opening the door of the cent shop to the public means opening a strictly regulated and exclusive 'aristocratic' space to the masses of customers regardless of their social rank, customers who even feel superior to the shopkeeper (41).

This 'democratization' or deregulation of the mansion's space can be read as a symbol of the democratizing influence that the changes of the nineteenth-century economic marketplace (allegedly) had. Therefore, in the next subchapter, I will use the image of the open shop door as a way to read *The House of the Seven Gables* first as a critical comment on the rapidly developing capitalist marketplace and the ways it changed the nation. Secondly, taking up Michael Gilmore's cue that "Hawthorne is using Hepzibah to express his own ambivalence about courting the public," I will read the romance as a somewhat more personal discussion of the situation Hawthorne as a writer might have faced on the literary marketplace.[7] Going beyond Gilmore's analysis, I will focus on the paradoxes and ambiguities such a reading entails, which become most obvious in how the romance ends.

2. Transgressions: Hepzibah Pyncheon and her "Pedestal of Imaginary Rank"

Hepzibah Pyncheon is one of the central, if not the central character in the novel.[8] In the development of her character, issues of gender and class intersect vis-à-vis the changing marketplace. Although she is part of the Pyncheon family, she herself is impoverished. Indeed, she is so poor that she seems to live on memories and illusions of her family's greatness rather than on any real food. Except for a lifelong title to the House of the Seven Gables she has virtually no possessions. This was not uncommon for women in the first half of the nineteenth century since traditional property laws favored male heirs over female ones.[9] Nevertheless, she has retained her independence, refusing, for instance, any help from her cousin Jaffrey. Although Hepzibah seems helpless and frail on first glance, her figure destroys the stereotype of the dependent woman. When her brother Clifford returns from his long imprisonment, she has to look for an additional source of income to support *him* and therefore decides to open a cent shop although it is a subject "of no slight mortification" (23) for her. The reason for this is laid out in detail by the narrator. Hepzibah is

> [a] lady – who had fed herself from childhood with the shadowy food of aristocratic reminiscences, and whose religion it was, that a lady's hand soils itself irremediably by doing aught for bread – this born lady, after sixty years of narrowing means, is fain to step down from her pedestal of imaginary rank. […] She must earn her own food, or starve! (29)

Despite her poverty, Hepzibah considers herself a lady, which is an essential part of her identity. Proud of her family's long-standing history, their wealth and the social position that comes with it, she carefully adheres to the norms and values of gentility and refinement, which are – among other things – signaled by leisure. Drawing on Thorstein Veblen's *The Theory of the Leisure Class*, Patrick Dooley points out that "[t]he inheritance of property, rather than its acquisition by other means, marks the true elite of the upper class." This supports the myth of an infinite abundance of wealth, which does not have to be earned.[10] Working for money, then, reveals the lack of wealth, and hence makes Hepzibah's claim to aristocratic gentility untenable.

Opening the actual shop door is significant in more than one way. It means the loss of Hepzibah's identity, whose ladylike hands become 'tainted' with the fact that she works, symbolized by the money that circulates through her fingers.[11] The outside realm intrudes into her make-belief world of aristocratic distinction and forces her to step down from what the narrator calls the "pedestal of imaginary rank" (29). Moreover, the open shop door is an interruption of her privacy, making her domestic and in a sense also her inner life public. Just as the nineteenth-century ideology of true womanhood saw the parlor as a mirror of the character of the inhabitants (linking, for instance, the objects displayed to the actual state of refinement of their owners), Hepzibah feels that with the opening of the shop her own innermost life is on display. The fact that she will be judged by the mundane (plebeian) working space of her cent shop rather than the more respectable (aristocratic) space of her parlor might make this even worse. Hepzibah becomes inevitably linked to the – rather pitiful-looking – commodities she displays in her shop window:

> She was well aware that she must ultimately come forward, and stand revealed in her proper individuality. [...] Nothing remained, except to take down the bar from the shop-door, leaving the entrance free – more than free – welcome, as if all were household friends – to every passer-by, whose eyes might be attracted by the commodities at the window. (31)

To be sure, the shop door goes two ways. Not only does it connect her to "the business of life" (24) but also allows the public to enter a house whose space has been regulated from the very beginning by a strict policy of class.[12] And indeed, it is particularly those customers Hepzibah perceives to be of lower class whose entrance she resents.[13] Her sense of distinction, which she imagined as "a gleam or halo of some kind or other, about her person" (41), is just that – an imagination on her part, for which other people do not care and which they neither recognize nor acknowledge.

The open shop door thus becomes a space of transition, a passageway which links Hepzibah to the outside world and allows the outside world to transgress into her space. It brings two different worlds into contact, 'anchoring' Hepzibah's cloudy aristocratic ideals in reality while demystifying the carefully hidden 'elite' space of the mansion for the (plebeian) masses at the same time. Significantly, it is little Ned Higgins, the perfect embodiment of the new consumer, with a voracious appetite and the money to finance it, who forces Hepzibah from "her pedestal of imaginary rank" (29) when she finally takes his money in return for a Jim Crow cookie.[14] On a metaphorical level, the encounter between Ned and Hepzibah illustrates that America's traditional social hierarchies had been changing in the first decades of the nineteenth century. A family's name no longer guaranteed one's place in society but rather financial success and achievement, turning conventional social hierarchies on their head.[15] Hepzibah's status as "old maid," her incompetence in the shop as well as her diminished status in society signal very clearly that she does not embody America's future, particularly as she is contrasted with little Ned, who displays the business sense of "a true-born Yankee" (39).

However, there is yet another way of reading Hepzibah, one connected to the *literary* marketplace. As I pointed out earlier, it is quite striking how Hepzibah delays the crossing of the threshold into the cent shop. As Susan Mizruchi argues, the narrator seems to procrastinate similarly in order to avoid the crossing of the threshold into his story proper, "loathe to begin a tale tainted by the profane details of commercial enterprise."[16] Such a link suggests that Hepzibah can be read as a stand-in for the author: Just as she is "aware that she must ultimately come forward, and stand revealed in her proper individuality" (31) in peddling her wares, the writer as well might feel that he reveals his inner self in presenting his literary goods to the public eye. As the narrator himself admits, "[a]ll this time, however, we are loitering faint-heartedly on the threshold of our story. In very truth, we have an invincible reluctance to disclose what Miss Hepzibah Pyncheon was about to do" (27). While witnessing and commenting upon Hepzibah's long-winded routine of getting ready to meet the eye and judgment of the public after her long seclusion, the narrator himself avoids the beginning of the story, 'hiding' it a bit longer from his readers' eyes.

The long preface, so typical of Hawthorne, can similarly be read as a way of putting off the beginning of the actual story. On the one hand, it claims to be an explanation to help the audience with the proper reading of the book (consider the novel's definition as "romance" and its "moral" mentioned here). On the other hand, the preface also seems confusing, not so much clarifying the deeper meaning of what is to follow than complicating it. Thus, the moment Hepzibah enters the world of commerce – her crossing over the threshold – becomes the moment that the author enters the world of commerce to peddle his romance and have it meet with the criticism of the public.[17] As Michael Gilmore astutely observes, Hawthorne "draws an implicit parallel between his writing and the commodities she hopes to sell," referring to "his book as an object to be eaten."[18] According to Hawthorne, the author "will be wise [...] to mingle the Marvellous rather as a slight, delicate and evanescent flavor, than as any portion of the actual substance of the dish offered to the Public" (3).

Another parallel underlines such a reading: Hepzibah's outward appearance links up metaphorically with Hawthorne's dark, gothic reputation. Her near-sightedness leads to her perpetual frowning, a scowl that has been misread as an outward sign of her inner unfriendliness and mistaken to be a generally negative attitude towards her environment. One could link her squinting to Hawthorne's scrutinizing look at America and its social, political, cultural, and ideological foundations. This critical and analytic inquiry has led to a reputation that assigns a dark, pessimistic outlook to the author and his work, a reputation which on closer inspection might be considered just as unjustified as Hepzibah's. What has been characterized as overly dark and pessimistic in Hawthorne's writing can also be understood as his 'scrutinizing squint,' his relentlessly open and critical dissecting of American society.

However, a number of details complicate this reading. To begin with, the narrator's own view of Hepzibah is quite ambiguous. Although he mocks her anxious, even hysterical behavior when opening her shop, the narrator can nevertheless relate to Hepzibah's fear of facing the public as can be seen in the parallel he draws between her commodities and his own literary wares. The procrastination discussed above also seems an indication for this. So is the surprisingly positive, even benign manner in which the narrator describes Hepzibah's enterprise in this chapter. However, the link between literary and shop commodities complicates such a reading. Hepzibah's outward appearance – the frown – is not the only problem she faces when trying to sell her goods. A lot of the items she carries are outdated, so old, in fact, that they are now of lesser quality. Her thread is "very rotten" (40). Her cookies are broken and "stale" (38), nothing more than "musty gingerbread" (29). While Hawthorne might have felt that his literary wares were outdated in the sense that they required an older sense of 'serious' literature and a related willingness to invest in reading it (in contrast to contemporary mass-produced texts), he probably did not think them to be 'stale' or deficient in quality.

Therefore, the parallels between Hepzibah and Hawthorne are not as straightforward as they seem. Hepzibah embodies the changes antebellum

America went through. Not all of them are as negative or problematic as the link between Hawthorne and Hepzibah might suggest. After all, her old and stale goods are later replaced by the fresh and better ones produced by Phoebe, which suggests that Hawthorne uses Hepzibah's struggle to highlight the democratizing forces and subsequent renewal of social structures – and hierarchies – as positive. Though he condemns her pretensions to social superiority, he might have secretly envied some of the privileges an aristocratic – i.e., independently financed – existence could have provided for himself, namely the possibility to concentrate on writing literature rather than on earning money with it. After all, Hepzibah as well as her brother Clifford are rewarded in the end with a carefree life of leisure.

3. Domesticating the Marketplace: Phoebe as 'Angel in the Shop'

Just as Hepzibah overcomes her hesitation and squeamishness, the narrator eventually crosses the threshold into his story, commenting on his contemporaries and their commitment to an increasingly profit-oriented marketplace. In his view, this threatens to destroy social balance and peace, and even democracy itself. Phoebe Pyncheon is one of the main figures with which he attempts to make his point. Significantly, she arrives on the day that Hepzibah opens her shop. If not to Hepzibah herself, then at least to the reader she seems an angel sent in order to help Hepzibah with her enterprise. Standing in front of the gloomy house, she is "widely in contrast […] with everything about her," comparable to "a ray of sunshine" that lights up the dismal place (51). Phoebe has rightly been read as the quintessential middle-class girl, the idealized version of the 'true woman.'[19] No sooner has she moved into the house than she endows it with "a look of comfort and habitableness," exorcizing the ghosts of the past with "a kind of natural magic" of her domestic skills (53). Moreover, conforming to the ideology of true womanhood, Phoebe's work is seemingly done effortlessly, even rendered invisible:

> Whatever she did, too, was done without conscious effort, and with frequent outbreaks of song […] finding joy in its activity and therefore rendering it beautiful; it was a New England trait – the stern old stuff of Puritanism, with a gold thread in the web. (56)

True to her name, then, Phoebe shines brightly in the domestic sphere. However, the "gold thread" that the narrator alludes to here can also be considered as a significant comment on Phoebe's ability in the cent shop. Her efforts are turned, if not into gold, at least into a "copper-mountain" (60).[20] Phoebe, who excels in the domestic sphere, also does extremely well in Hepzibah's cent shop. Her domestic skills are in part responsible for her success. The gift for arranging the commodities, her skills of production (the yeast, the cakes, the beer etc.), and the friendliness and positive attitude with which she takes care of the customers are all grounded in her sense of domesticity.

Hence, Phoebe stands in utter contrast to Hepzibah, who notes more than once that "Phoebe is no Pyncheon" (59) and, moreover, no lady. Phoebe's "new Plebeianism" is opposed to Hepzibah's "old Gentility" since she is "a true New England woman" aiming "to seek her fortune, but with a self-respecting purpose to confer as much benefit as she could anywise receive" (54). Moreover, she herself declares "I mean to earn my bread. […] A girl learns many things in a New England village" (55). She is therefore the matching counterpart to the proverbial nineteenth-century self-made man. However, Phoebe's sense of business and her ambition are held in check by the desire to reciprocate her success, to pay back the "benefit" she earned in the business world. Hence, while being 'at home' in the world of enterprise, for which the cent shop stands, Phoebe is not simply profit-oriented, despite her sense of business. She not only uses the new opportunities offered by the market but domesticates the market in turn, showing the necessity to tame the forces of profit-orientation. In the logic of the novel, this can be achieved by the female middle-class norms and values she personifies.

The idealized figure of Phoebe does not merely stand for the new middle classes, their relation to the capitalist marketplace, and the necessity to tame its potentially destructive forces. Like Hepzibah, Phoebe could be read in a way that extends the image of economic transactions to the business of writing. Just as Hepzibah might be a reference to the author, Phoebe could be seen as an embodiment of his audience.[21] It is telling that Phoebe, as Hepzibah's opposite and the only character in the novel who manages to be pure and virtuous while actually participating successfully in the new market economy, does not signify the writer – as if Hawthorne felt the new economic structures to be incompatible with true art and literature. The remarkable contrast between Hepzibah and Phoebe, then, underscores the rupture Hawthorne might have felt between his work and what he perceived as the vulgar, even 'trashy' taste of the masses. Hawthorne's infamous quote I alluded to above ends with the declaration that "I should have no chance of success while the public taste is occupied with their trash [i.e., the scribbling women's books] – and should be ashamed of myself if I did succeed."[22] Put differently, and in the terms of the novel, Hepzibah – the writer – is out of tune with the present and, especially, the contemporary audience's new taste and preferences for commodities, in this case the literary text. In this context, Hepzibah's nostalgic longing for the past, a kind of escapism from what she feels to be an unbearable present, would signify the author's preference for an older, less profit-oriented literary market.[23] Phoebe, as part of the young and increasingly influential new generation, embodies such different tastes – in addition to her knack for knowing what customers would like to buy, she herself likes to go shopping and also enjoys the occasional lecture, likewise a fairly new form of entertainment for the middle classes that connects the new desire for leisure and consumption with older ideas of intellectual and spiritual self-improvement.

One scene most explicitly supports such a reading of Phoebe as the embodiment of the new, mid-century (mass) audience and its tastes. It is Holgrave's reading of his story "Alice Pyncheon," which he intends to publish (chapter 13). His allusion to *Graham's Magazine* as well as *Godey's Lady's Book* (133) not only emphasizes his literary ambition. As two of the leading and most popular magazines of the time, *Graham's* and *Godey's* are references to the literary mass market. His choice reveals an acute business sense of where to publish his stories. Moreover, it directly connects him to Hawthorne himself, who had published in both magazines.[24] Yet it is also telling that Holgrave works mainly as a daguerreotypist, producing pictures that were by many considered to be only a 'second-rate' art-form, especially in contrast to literature. This would suggest that he is not so much a 'true' writer as a commercially oriented artist, at least as far as nineteenth-century evaluations go.[25]

Phoebe's reaction to this story is quite enlightening. She agrees to listen to his story "if it is not very long [...] nor very dull!" (133), a clear indication of her preferences and abilities as a reader. What is more, during the reading Phoebe almost falls asleep. Whether this is due to the mesmerizing quality of Holgrave's writing or Phoebe's short attention span and lack of interest remains open. Nevertheless, Phoebe's comment on the story afterwards is quite instructive in terms of her (lack of) understanding: "I consider myself as having been very attentive; and though I don't remember the incidents quite distinctly, yet I have an impression of a vast deal of trouble and calamity" (151). This is clearly also the author's comment on the attention span, the literary perception and sensitivity as well as the taste of an audience, whom he considered more and more given over to the mass-produced literature that sold so well but that he considered to be "trash."[26] Trained by what literary magazines and newspapers offered to their readers, the audience, exemplified by Phoebe here, no longer grasps – nor cares for – any deeper meaning that literary texts might have to offer.[27] "[T]rouble" and "calamity" are the keywords here, maybe exemplifying both an increasingly sensationalist and an overly sentimental character of literature (at least as it was perceived by Hawthorne).

While Phoebe is one of the figures who successfully negotiate the changed demands of the marketplace, she also exemplifies the pressure that these changes brought to the literary sphere. Name and rank alone no longer guarantee readership or success. Not only does the writer have to make a name for him- or herself (which Hawthorne certainly had by the time he published *The House of the Seven Gables*). He (or she) also has to be financially successful in an increasingly competitive literary market. As an embodiment of middle-class virtues, Phoebe integrates both the successful negotiation and the domestication of the new economic realities American society faced and emerges as a positive image for the democratizing forces the new economic opportunities made possible. Yet this also has a negative side to it as far as the democratization of literary taste goes. If the market was ruled by the literary preferences of the masses, there seems to be no place for 'unpopular' (in the sense of potentially critical and discomforting) literature. Any writer who needs to be successful in the competitive realm of literature has to pay attention to such market rules, even if they go against his or her artistic sensitivities. Hence, it is not surprising that Phoebe, an embodiment of the new literary marketplace, has thoroughly 'tamed' the artist and writer Holgrave and his radical ideas by the end of the novel. This also signifies Hawthorne's own sense that his literary ideals might be in danger of 'domestication' by his readership and their (new) taste.[28]

4. Moving Out: Reading the Ending of *The House of the Seven Gables*

The somewhat abrupt ending of Hawthorne's novel, with its surprising and rather unrealistic character, has been seen as unsatisfactory, especially by twentieth- and twenty-first-century readers.[29] Its constructed nature has frequently been read as the author's attempt to make his novel seem somewhat brighter than its predecessor *The Scarlet Letter*.[30] While this might well be the case, I would like to argue that the constructed nature of the ending also reflects Hawthorne's deep-seated ambiguity regarding the economic changes, both their democratizing and their potentially corrupting influence, which affected not just the nation as a whole and its literary market.

Traditionally, fictional endings dish out rewards and punishment. In the case of *The House of the Seven Gables*, Judge Pyncheon, representative of the overly powerful, wealthy, and greedy aristocracy, dies and with him the whole family line. With Hepzibah and Clifford Pyncheon both unmarried and too old for offspring anyway, the novel's ending envisions – apparently – the end of what had until now been the elite ruling class in America: old, landed gentry, who relied on their social connections and wealth to remain powerful and increase their material resources to the disadvantage of the lower classes. The last offspring of the Pyncheons, Phoebe, is of course still around. However, she never was a 'true' Pyncheon and thus never had their ill-formed sense of inherited superiority. Coming from a mixed-class background, she takes everything from her middle-class mother (to echo Hepzibah's thoughts). Moreover, she continues what one could call the transgression of class boundaries as she will marry Holgrave, the working-class lad with promising skill and talent. Apart from this, the marriage between Holgrave and Phoebe is also symbolically significant since it will effectively put an end to the ancient feud between the aristocratic Pyncheons and the working-class Maule family, setting right an age-old crime based on class inequality. In this regard, the ending is a celebration of the idea of a classless society, of equality and upward mobility, which were influential ideas during the nineteenth century. Somewhat paradoxically, though ideologically significant, this classlessness becomes embodied by the new middle classes and their ideals.[31] Thus, in the end, the deserving are rewarded and more than well taken care of. Clifford, unjustly imprisoned, comes to enjoy his rightful heritage. So does his sister Hepzibah, who stood by him. Phoebe and

Holgrave are rewarded for their industry and enterprising spirit. And even Uncle Venner, the pauper, is in a true charitable manner taken care of as all of the characters leave the old House of the Seven Gables to move into Judge Pyncheon's more modern and more comfortable country estate.[32]

Such a reading is fraught with ambiguities and seems to raise more questions than it answers.[33] The most pressing one surely concerns Hawthorne's dislike of inherited privilege, money, and power. Why did he reward Phoebe and Holgrave, the two characters fit best for the new economic marketplace, precisely with such a heritage? Similarly, why is Hepzibah allowed to live a genteel (and unproductive) life of leisure, which thus reinforces her sense of imaginary superiority? I would suggest that this is part of the actually 'unhappy' vision that Hawthorne's romance ends with. As Amy Lang so aptly observes, "the 'lower classes' as Hepzibah styles them, seem always to lose on their investments, while the aristocracy, whose demise the novel ostensibly recounts, are fortuitously saved from poverty."[34] In the end, Hepzibah's enterprise, even without her own work, turned into what the envious, surprised working-class man Dixey calls "pretty good business," a success that stands in striking contrast to that of his friend's wife, who lost "five dollars on her outlay" for a cent shop (225). In this sense, Hawthorne clearly draws attention to the fact that while America's burgeoning new economy might open up numerous possibilities for economic success, these possibilities are not equally open to everyone. Rather, despite nourishing the myth of endless possibilities provided one is only industrious and clever enough – Benjamin Franklin's self-made man – the system favors, in fact, those who already profit from the system, through money, connections, and education.

In the end, despite Judge Pyncheon's death, not much has changed and thus, the ending might not be as happy as it is usually taken to be. The estate, which could be seen as a location of both political and financial power (after all, the Judge wanted to become the next governor of Massachusetts), is now shared by inhabitants of different classes. In other words, power, traditionally reserved to the aristocratic classes (the governing elite in the Jeffersonian sense), is now extended to the middle classes as personified by Phoebe and Holgrave. However, Holgrave's rebellious character has been thoroughly domesticated by Phoebe and not much seems to be left of his will to change society in any radical way.[35] His will to tear down solid houses (131), signifying his desire for reform, change, and renewal, has suddenly been replaced by a preference for "permanence, which [he] consider[s] essential to the happiness of any one moment" (222). Moreover, Uncle Venner, the pauper, is only admitted on charity, as a guest so to speak. Therefore, the lower classes do not really have access to power unless they are invited by those who have. In a sense, women are 'left outside' as well: their independence attained in the successful cent shop is exchanged for a dependence upon brother and husband, since it is the men who will have access to the fortune as Eva Boesenberg has rightly pointed out.[36] In this sense, Hawthorne might have made the ending *apparently* a happier one, in order to sell his literary commodity all the better to his audience. Considering the ambiguous, even contradictory nature that the ending has, we can assume that what he, in fact, sold them, was a vision of America's future that on closer inspection seems much bleaker.

Notes

[1] Richard Fox and Jackson Lears (1983), for instance, speak of a shift from "a nineteenth-century 'producer ethic'" towards a "dominant twentieth-century 'consumer ethic'" (x [ix-xvii]). The whole story of America's economic transformation is of course much more complex. It could be argued for instance that the American economy has been 'capitalist' from its very beginnings. See e.g. Larson (2010), 3. A number of scholars have also convincingly argued that, even before the nineteenth century, Americans were far less self-subsistent and more oriented towards consumption than they are usually assumed to be. See Shammas (1990) and Breen (2004). Nevertheless, economic changes were so dramatic during the nineteenth century that historians speak of a "market revolution." Cf. Sellers (1991). A more concise account can be found in Larson (2010).

[2] Stuart M. Blumin (1989). *The Emergence of the Middle Class: Social Experience in the American City, 1760-1900.* Cambridge: Cambridge University Press; Richard L. Bushman (1993 [1992]). *The Refinement of America: Persons, Houses, Cities.* New York: Vintage Books. See also Merish (2000), Smith (2002), Nelson (2004), and Shi (1985).

[3] Nathaniel Hawthorne (2006 [1851]). *The House of the Seven Gables*. Ed. Robert S. Levine. New York: Norton. Further references to this edition will be included in the text.

[4] Poe's gothic house has, for instance, likewise a human countenance with "vacant eye-like windows" (138, 139 [138-157]). Also cf. Michael Davitt Bell (1995),

who suggests that "the ending of *The House of the Seven Gables* [could be described] as a domestic revision of the ending of 'The Fall of the House of Usher,'" suggesting that Hawthorne's novel makes a transition from the gothic novel to the domestic one (117).

[5] For an excellent and extensive discussion of *The House* in relation to Hawthorne and his profession as a writer see Gilmore (1981). While I agree in many points with his argument, my own reading differs in various points from his, especially regarding the ending.

[6] The complete quote reads: "Besides, America is now wholly given over to a d——d mob of scribbling women, and I should have no chance of success while the public taste is occupied with their trash – and should be ashamed of myself if I did succeed. What is the mystery of these innumerable editions of the Lamplighter, and other books neither better nor worse? – worse they could not be, and better they need not be, when they sell by the 100,000" (Hawthorne (1987), 304 [303-305]). This was written on 19 January 1855 in a letter that Hawthorne sent to his publisher William D. Ticknor. For a discussion of the quote see Baym (1999).

[7] Gilmore (1981), 176.

[8] Cf. Baym (2004), who convincingly argues that Hepzibah can be seen as the protagonist of the novel.

[9] One of the reasons for this was certainly that a woman's property went to her husband when she married and thus was lost to the family. On women's economic legal rights see for instance Warren (2005), particularly chapter two; Salmon (1989); and Weyler (2009), particularly pages 3-10.

[10] Patrick K. Dooley (1980). "Genteel Poverty: Hepzibah in *The House of the Seven Gables*." *The Markham Review* 9, 33 (33-35). Robert K. Martin (1998) calls this the "upper-class claim to the invisibility of money's origins" (133), which hides the fact that a large part of New England wealth was based on the economy of slavery (134).

[11] Just as she postpones opening the shop, she also avoids touching the money as long as she can. Even later on when she has to count her proceeds from the day, Hepzibah is wearing gloves "so as not to contaminate herself" (121) as Teresa Goddu (1991) points out.

[12] Cf. the novel's first chapter, which describes Colonel Pyncheon's festivities to celebrate the completion of his mansion.

[13] Not surprisingly, Hepzibah perceives such lower-class customers particularly in terms of their bodily dimensions, especially odor and sound, which intrude upon her delicate senses: For instance, "there was an encounter, just at the door-step, betwixt two laboring men, as their rough voices denoted them to be" (36), who comment negatively on her attempt to open the shop; another "man in the blue cotton-frock, much soiled, came in and bought a pipe; filling the whole shop, meanwhile, with the hot odor of strong drink [...] oozing out of his entire system,

like an inflammable gas" (40); and finally she encounters the "round, bustling, fire-ruddy housewife, of the neighborhood, [who] burst breathless into the shop, fiercely demanding yeast" and who is outraged that Hepzibah carries none (40-41).

[14] The scene is, of course, also highly significant with regard to the consumption of race, which I cannot discuss here. For a reading of Hawthorne's *House* in terms of its racial economies see e.g. Martin (1998); and Anthony (1999).

[15] See for instance Walter T. Herbert (2004), who reads the novel in the context of a shift from a society in which everybody's place was defined by birth to one in which new economic opportunities provided at least the chance of upward mobility regardless of birth.

[16] Susan Mizruchi (1988). "From History to Gingerbread: Manufacturing a Republic in *The House of the Seven Gables*." *The Power of Historical Knowledge: Narrating the Past in Hawthorne, James, and Dreiser*. Princeton: Princeton University Press, 90 (83-134).

[17] Cf. Baym (2004), who also draws this parallel between Hepzibah and Hawthorne: "Soon to abandon fifteen years of hermit-like privacy to open a shop (like her author, we might say, issuing from his Salem attic to offer his literary wares to the public), Hepzibah is in a paroxysm of comical nervousness" (609). His letters to his publisher Fields during the last months before the book's publication allude to unexpected difficulties in finishing it, maybe an indication for the author's anxiety to reveal his latest work. See Charvat (1965), xvii-xviii.

[18] Gilmore (1981), 177.

[19] See, for instance, Lang (2003), 37-38; Millington (1992), 116; and Pfister (1991), 151.

[20] Similarly, the image of the gold thread is repeated later on in a comment on "women's office to move in the midst of practical affairs, and to gild them all [...] with an atmosphere of loveliness and joy" (59), a gilding touch that can also be read in economic terms with regard to Phoebe.

[21] And it is, of course, interesting that Hawthorne chooses to use female characters to symbolize the relation of author and audience, reflecting first of all on the fact that a large number of writers earning money with their writing were women and secondly, that the burgeoning literary market – at least in the fictional area – was to a large extent ruled by the taste of a largely female audience.

[22] Hawthorne (1987), 304.

[23] Susan Mizruchi (1988) sees Hepzibah as "incompatible with the demands of the present, which leads her to fantasize a past over which her imaginative control might be complete," a fantasy which is underlined by the "family ornaments" distributed all over the house (90).

[24] Gilmore (1981), 180. Holgrave's self-ironic comment on his own qualities as a writer is ambiguous here: "In the humorous line, I am thought to have a very pretty way with me; and as for pathos, I am as provocative of tears as an onion!" (133)

Clearly, humor and, especially, pathos are the key to (his) success but "a very pretty way" and the reference to an onion are hardly artistic evaluations of these qualities. For a reading of Holgrave as an artist figure see Baym (1970).

[25] Again, this point is complicated on closer inspection. In contrast to such a 'mechanistic' view of daguerreotypy, Holgrave claims that he is able to go beyond the "surface" of things with the help of the daguerreotype as "it actually brings out the secret character [of the sitter] with a truth that no painter would ever venture upon, even could he detect it. There is at least no flattery in my humble line of art" (67). Such a claim becomes especially interesting considering the fact that Holgrave hides his own identity as a descendent of Maule. Cf. Davidson (1990), 688. Moreover, considering the visual quality of the daguerreotype – it showed both a positive and a negative image of the portrayed as well as a reflection of the viewer on its shiny surface depending on the viewer's viewpoint (Davidson (1990), 681) – one could argue that such a claim to truthfulness is based on 'ambiguity' and not on a mechanistic mimesis. For more extended discussions of the art of daguerreotypy in the novel see Dinius (2012), Kley (2009), and Trachtenberg (2000).

[26] Hawthorne (1987), 304.

[27] Cf. Anthony (1999), who reads this scene as a "didactic lesson about the powers of mass culture" and the "putatively regressive effects" it has (259).

[28] See Davidson (1990), who reads Holgrave's 'conversion' as "a symbolic artistic suicide" closely related to Hawthorne's own anxieties as a writer (691). See Baym (1970) for a different reading of Holgrave as an artist. She argues as well that his change in the end is decidedly not a happy or positive one but reads it as a sign for his entrapment in the forces of history, the fact that he cannot escape Judge Pyncheon in the end (595).

[29] Davidson (1990), 691; Davidson observes that "[i]t is tacked on, like the denouement of the worst kind of melodrama." See also Gilmore (1981), 172.

[30] Charvat (1965), for instance, writes that "[t]he denouement of the story must also be considered a professional problem," suggesting that Hawthorne was "yielding to the world's wish that in stories everything should turn out well" (xxi).

[31] See Lang (2003), who argues that the prominence of gender relations helps to hide the significance of class in *The House of the Seven Gables*.

[32] Interestingly, this is a move that leads everybody from a quarter of the town that has become less fashionable over the years to the more beautiful (and less crowded) countryside. Leaving the place that has by now become run-over by the lower classes, the characters withdraw (again) to a more exclusive surrounding.

[33] Gilmore (1981), for instance, states that Hawthorne "evidently overlooked his own warnings about the evils of inheritance" (172).

[34] Lang (2003), 32.

[35] See Dinius (2012) for a different reading of the ending that links radicalism and conservatism (65-67).

[36] Eva Boesenberg (2010). "Money and the Ideology of Separate Spheres in Novels of the 1850s." *Money and Gender in the American Novel, 1850-2000.* Heidelberg: Winter, 70 (61-131).

Bibliography

Anthony, David (1999). "Class, Culture, and the Trouble with White Skin in Hawthorne's *The House of the Seven Gables.*" *The Yale Journal of Criticism* 12.2, 249-268.

Baym, Nina (2004). "The Heroine of *The House of the Seven Gables*; Or, Who Killed Jaffrey Pyncheon?" *The New England Quarterly* 77.4, 607-618.

--- (1999). "Again and Again, the Scribbling Women." *Hawthorne and Women: Engendering and Expanding the Hawthorne Tradition.* Eds. John L. Idol, Jr. and Melinda M. Ponder. Boston: University of Massachusetts Press, 20-35.

--- (1970). "Hawthorne's Holgrave: The Failure of the Artist-Hero." *The Journal of English and Germanic Philology* 69.4, 584-598.

Bell, Michael Davitt (1995). "Women's Fiction and the Literary Marketplace in the 1850s." *The Cambridge History of American Literature.* Vol. 2. Ed. Sacvan Bercovitch. Cambridge: Cambridge University Press, 74-123.

Blumin, Stuart M. (1989). *The Emergence of the Middle Class: Social Experience in the American City, 1760-1900.* Cambridge: Cambridge University Press.

Boesenberg, Eva (2010). "Money and the Ideology of Separate Spheres in Novels of the 1850s." *Money and Gender in the American Novel, 1850-2000.* Heidelberg: Winter, 61-131.

Breen, T. H. (2004). *The Marketplace of Revolution: How Consumer Politics Shaped American Independence.* Oxford: Oxford University Press.

Bushman, Richard L. (1993 [1992]). *The Refinement of America: Persons, Houses, Cities.* New York: Vintage Books.

Charvat, William (1965). "Introduction to *The House of the Seven Gables.*" *The House of the Seven Gables. The Centenary Edition of the Works of Nathaniel Hawthorne.* Vol. II. Eds. W. C. et al. Columbus: Ohio State University Press, xv-xxviii.

Davidson, Cathy N. (1990). "Photographs of the Dead: Sherman, Daguerre, Hawthorne." *South Atlantic Quarterly* 89.4, 667-701.

Dinius, Marcy J. (2012). "Daguerreian Romanticism: *The House of the Seven Gables* and Gabriel Harrison's Portraits." *The Camera and the Press: American Visual Culture and Print Culture in the Age of the Daguerreotype.* Philadelphia: University of Pennsylvania Press, 49-85.

Dooley, Patrick K. (1980). "Genteel Poverty: Hepzibah in *The House of the Seven Gables.*" *The Markham Review* 9, 33-35.

Fox, Richard Wightman, and T. J. Jackson Lears (1983). "Introduction." *The Culture of Consumption: Critical Essays in American History, 1880-1980*. Eds. R. W. F. and T. J. J. L. New York: Pantheon, ix-xvii.

Gilmore, Michael (1981). "The Artist in the Marketplace in the House of the Seven Gables." *EHL* 48.1, 172-189.

Goddu, Teresa (1991). "The Circulation of Women in *The House of the Seven Gables*." *Studies in the Novel* 23.1, 119-127.

Hawthorne, Nathaniel (2006 [1851]). *The House of the Seven Gables*. Ed. Robert S. Levine. New York: Norton.

--- (1987). "Letter to William D. Ticknor, January 19, 1855. *The Letters, 1853-1856*." *The Centenary Edition of the Works of Nathaniel Hawthorne*. Vol. XVII. Eds. Thomas Woodson et al. Columbus: Ohio State University Press, 303-305.

Herbert, Walter T. (2004). "Hawthorne and American Masculinity." *The Cambridge Companion to Nathaniel Hawthorne*. Ed. Richard H. Millington. Cambridge: Cambridge University Press, 60-78.

Kley, Antje (2009). *Ethik medialer Repräsentation im britischen und US-amerikanischen Roman, 1741-2000*. Heidelberg: Winter.

Lang, Amy Schrager (2003). "Home, in the Better Sense: The Model Woman, the Middle Class, and the Harmony of Interests." *The Syntax of Class: Writing Inequality in Nineteenth-Century American Literature*. Princeton: Princeton University Press, 14-41.

Larson, John Lauritz (2010). *The Market Revolution in America: Liberty, Ambition, and the Eclipse of the Common Good*. Cambridge: Cambridge University Press.

Martin, Robert K. (1998). "Haunted by Jim Crow: Gothic Fictions by Hawthorne and Faulkner." *American Gothic: New Interventions in a National Narrative*. Eds. R. K. M. and Eric Savoy. Iowa City: University of Iowa Press, 129-142.

Matthiesen, F. O. (1968 [1941]). "Hawthorne's Politics, with the Economic Structure of *The Seven Gables*." *American Renaissance: Art and Expression in the Age of Emerson and Whitman*. London: Oxford University Press, 316-337.

Merish, Lori (2000). *Sentimental Materialism: Gender, Commodity Culture, and Nineteenth-Century American Literature*. Durham: Duke University Press.

Millington, Richard H. (1992). "Romance as Engagement: *The House of the Seven Gables*." *Practicing Romance: Narrative Form and Cultural Engagement in Hawthorne's Fiction*. Princeton: Princeton University Press, 105-153.

Mizruchi, Susan (1988). "From History to Gingerbread: Manufacturing a Republic in *The House of the Seven Gables*." *The Power of Historical Knowledge: Narrating the Past in Hawthorne, James, and Dreiser*. Princeton: Princeton University Press, 83-134.

Nelson, Elizabeth White (2004). *Market Sentiments: Middle-Class Market Culture in Nineteenth-Century America*. Washington: Smithsonian.

Pfister, Joel (1991). "Cleaning House: From the Gothic Order to the Middle-Class World Order." *The Production of Personal Life: Class, Gender, and the Psychological in Hawthorne's Fiction.* Stanford: Stanford University Press, 144-161.

Poe, Edgar Allan (1986). "The Fall of the House of Usher." *The Fall of the House of Usher and Other Writings.* New York: Penguin, 138-157.

Salmon, Marylynn (1989). "Republican Sentiment, Economic Change, and the Property Rights of Women in American Law." *Women in the Age of the American Revolution.* Eds. Ronald Hoffman and Peter J. Albert. Charlottesville: University Press of Virginia, 447-475.

Sellers, Charles (1991). *The Market Revolution: Jacksonian America, 1815-1846.* New York: Oxford University Press.

Shammas, Carole (1990). *The Pre-industrial Consumer in England and America.* Oxford: Clarendon.

Shi, David E. (1985). *The Simple Life: Plain Living and High Thinking in American Culture.* New York: Oxford University Press.

Smith, Woodruff D. (2002). *Consumption and the Making of Respectability, 1600-1800.* New York: Routledge.

Trachtenberg, Alan (2000). "Seeing and Believing: Hawthorne's Reflections on the Daguerreotype in *The House of the Seven Gables.*" *National Imaginaries, American Identities: The Cultural Work of American Iconography.* Eds. Larry J. Reynolds and Gordon Hutner. Princeton: Princeton University Press, 31-51.

Warren, Joyce W. (2005). *Women, Money and the Law: Nineteenth-Century Fiction, Gender, and the Courts.* Iowa City: University of Iowa Press.

Weyler, Karen A. (2009). "Marriage, Coverture, and the Companionate Ideal in *The Coquette* and *Dorval.*" *Legacy* 26.1, 1-25.

Christoph Ribbat (Paderborn)

"Where Do You Get Your Daguerreotypes?" Image, Text, Race, and a Nineteenth-Century Businessman

1. Consumption Meets Iconophobia: Reading Race in the Eighteen-Fifties

In a consumer society, everything hinges on advertising. Even in antebellum America, before department stores and national brands, commercial notices were everywhere.[1] Hence it is only appropriate to look at an ad in order to open this exploration of consumption, race, image, and text in the mid-nineteenth-century United States. In 1854, the readers of the *Cincinnati Enquirer* came across this imaginary dialogue between two local citizens. "Where do you get your Daguerreotypes?" an Ohioan asks. "At Ball's," another person answers, referring to James Presley Ball, the photographer running the notice. "Why do you get them there?" the curious consumer inquires again. "For four reasons, as follows," the interviewee replies in a tone perhaps more mechanical than convincing. "His pictures are most lifelike; They are the most beautiful; They are the most durable; And they are the cheapest."[2]

It is not surprising that the "lifelike" quality of Ball's images is first on the mind of this fictional expert. The nineteenth century offers particularly rich examples of photography's close connection to the real, however problematic that notion may be. Writers constantly reminded their readers of the astonishingly accurate images that cameras produced. Authors ranging from Edgar Allan Poe and Nathaniel Hawthorne to William Dean Howells and Henry James commented on photography, turned photographers into protagonists, and juggled visual terms when theorizing the art of writing. Realist fiction and the medium of photography developed in the same historical moment. They appear to have been mutually dependent on each other. As Nancy Armstrong shows, photography constituted what was 'real' about realism.[3] Nonetheless, nineteenth-century authors often refer to photography in pejorative terms. In contrast to literature, seen as nuanced and complex, writers portray camera work as limited and limiting, even morally dubious.[4] Surely this thread is not picked up in the *Cincinnati Enquirer*'s advertisement. Like many other early observers of photography, the imaginary expert praising James Presley Ball's works refers to their "beautiful" (qtd. in: Willis, "Introduction," xvi) features. But the medium's status was precarious. The new images seemed aesthetically pleasing to some, mechanical and superficial to others.[5]

The fickle reputation of photographs can be traced back to their role in consumer culture. Glancing at this 1854 advertisement, the *Cincinnati Enquirer's* readers will have noted that James Presley Ball's images were "the most durable" and "the cheapest" (qtd. in: Willis, "Introduction," xvi). Photographs functioned as commodities. Their durability and their price mattered. Considering novels as consumer products could be seen as an (albeit extremely important) second analytical step taken by literary historians. In contrast, photography was a business first, unequivocally so. Daguerreotypists roamed rural and small-town America. They carried their equipment to anyone who could afford to have their portraits taken. In the cities, galleries displayed pictures and offered their services.[6] Nathaniel Hawthorne's *House of the Seven Gables* testifies to the significance of the daguerreotypist in mid-nineteenth-century American literature and culture.

Because photography, like advertising, was omnipresent, portraiture, once the domain of the society's elite, turned into a middle-class practice.[7] New York entrepreneurs like Mathew Brady and Napoleon Sarony displayed photos of celebrities and historical events. Showing off luxurious props and backgrounds, their studios and galleries became temples of consumerism. While most customers would pay to be photographed, some subjects – the most famous actresses of their time, for instance – would be paid for sitting. Fame itself thus turned into a product, broadening the scope of consumption. Operating in a century of rapidly improving printing technologies and a mass market for images, new photo-businessmen shaped visual culture. Miles Orvell finds the roots "of our obsessively voyeuristic society" in the photography galleries of the nineteenth century.[8] In a broader sense, the portraitists marketed a new mode to perform and conceive of middle-class selves. Their customers may have believed that they could find their true identity, and the identity of their loved ones, in the images they ordered and purchased.[9]

James Presley Ball was a businessman, then, and certainly a highly successful one. A journalist described one of his enterprises, named "Ball's Great Daguerrean Gallery of the West," as a "flourishing business." Another observer marveled at the proprietor's "indomitable industry" that led to "the great increase of his business" (qtd. in: Willis, "Introduction," xvi).

But we should discuss another detail. James Presley Ball, the producer of lifelike, beautiful, durable and cheap images, was African American: a free black man in antebellum America. This did not go unnoticed. Reporting from Ohio, a black journalist working for an abolitionist newspaper commented on the "variety of employments engaged in by colored men" in the city of Cincinnati. He praised "Mr. Ball" and his "magnificent Daguerrean Gallery" as "one of the best answers to the charge of natural inferiority we [i.e., African Americans] have lately met with" (qtd. in: Willis, "Introduction," xv). The statement, however brief, raises highly interesting questions. In the 1850s United States, a nation caught in a political crisis leading up to the Civil War, race was the key issue of the time. Obviously, it was James Presley Ball's craft to represent human beings in photographs. But he was working in a national context in which the very question whether African Americans should be seen as human beings and potential citizens or as possessions, things, and commodities was still unresolved.

As we shall see, Ball consciously reflected on these matters: first as a photographer, second as an entrepreneur combining spectacle and abolitionist ideas. Before turning to this case study, it seems necessary to unpack the methodological complexities that make Ball such a fascinating figure. These questions take us back to the dynamic relations of image, text, and race. More precisely, they lead to the intertwined histories of literary and visual culture. One of these histories clearly stands out. Compared to any sort of image, literature appears to provide the more complex and nuanced representations of non-white antebellum subjects. In the *Norton Anthology of African American Literature*, a standard text, the slave narrative appears as the key genre of its period, "America's only indigenous literary form," its scope far exceeds its anti-slavery agenda. In the slave narrative, literary historians argue, authors established "self-awareness, intellectual independence and literary authority."[10] The autobiographical texts connected between African American oral traditions and Euro-American literary culture.[11] If we see the "dedication to human dignity" as the "sustaining spirit of African American literature,"[12] the literary work – say by Frederick Douglass or Harriet Jacobs – constitutes the most important terrain dignity will unfold in. Slave narratives were consumer objects, too. Douglass's first autobiography, for instance, selling for 50 cents in the eighteen-forties, 30,000 curious readers bought in the first decade of its circulation on the American and British markets.[13] Nonetheless, we trust the literary text to provide the richest possible narrative.

In stark contrast, scholars have shown how visual culture, i.e., the commerce in images, photographs, and popular spectacles, was entangled with the most vicious forms of racism the nineteenth century produced. African American writers and thinkers hence reflected on vision as "a hostile realm of significance."[14] At the time that Frederick Douglass's first slave narrative stunned American readers, cartoonists, photographers, and minstrel show actors caricatured the black body and the black face as grotesque and primitive. Photography helped establish the 'science' of race. From these representations, a "visual-biological determinism" emerged.[15] In another cultural register, North and South collaborated in producing images supporting the system of slavery. Printers in Northern cities created images of runaway slaves for the Southern market. In the period following the 1850 Fugitive Slave Act, these typographic characters circulated in the entire Union. The image of the escaped slave became a "standard element" of American culture.[16] In the realm of entertainment, the minstrel show drew its power on the cultural marketplace not simply from the way performers caricatured African Americans, but from a broad variety of visual effects designed to reinforce the alleged duality of white and black.[17] In the eighteen-thirties, P. T. Barnum, arguably the most important creator of commercialized cultural spectacle, toured the United States with his "Greatest Natural and National Curiosity in the World." Barnum displayed a woman named Joice Heth, a supposedly 161-year old former slave of George Washington.[18] The heavy circulation of images and the accelerating processes of American consumer culture overlapped. Late nineteenth-century visual culture would produce "commodity racism": material artifacts that were racially coded.[19] The matrix for such products was established in the antebellum years.

Even in abolitionist media, the figure of the suffering slave loomed as a de-individualized standard emblem. As Michael Chaney notes, these anti-slavery "counterimages" tended to be voyeuristic and "reductive."

The cliché of black suffering turned into a staple of antebellum consumer culture. Images of victimized slaves appeared on toys, on pillows, and on plates.[20] Whereas the privacy of the white middle-class family was considered sacrosanct, the black body, tortured and on display, reinforced fictions of unquestionable white privilege and distinction.[21] The most widely-read abolitionist novel, *Uncle Tom's Cabin* inspired a multitude of racist images. Marcus Wood identifies Stowe's bestseller as "a culture in which the bacteria of nineteenth-century racism flourished." Wood points to the "racist commonplaces which infested [the novel's] adapted visual forms."[22]

Images thus played a central role in producing and expressing nineteenth-century racism. This has led to a form of iconophobia prevalent in literary and cultural criticism. Images present bodies. Hence, they seem to "occlude the subjects inhabiting specific bodies." As Nancy Armstrong shows, they make us "hostile to visual representation" as such.[23] But there are good reasons to reconsider this aversion.

2. The Consumer's Pose: Antebellum Portraits of African Americans

In recent years, American literary and cultural historians have called for a more nuanced view of antebellum visual culture and its representations of race. Photography historian Deborah Willis not only rescued James Presley Ball's work from obscurity. Over decades of archival research, Willis produced a canon of African American photography, reaching back to the earliest years of the medium.[24] Following in Willis's footsteps, Maurice Wallace and Shawn Michelle Smith critique the over-emphasis on white clichéd representation. They state that "we know more about the imagery of racism than we do about what African American men and women did when they took photography into their own hands." And they urge Americanists to consider the diverse objects and commodities circulating in the national culture: daguerreotypes, tintypes, cartes de visite, and the way these were used in black struggles for "new social positions and political identities."[25]

Portrait of Elizabeth Ball Thomas, daughter of Thomas Ball. Ca. 1850s, Daguerreotype, sixth plate (from: Willis [*J. P. Ball*, 1993], 10).

Portrait of an unidentified black man seated in a chair, wearing a bow tie and high-button jacket. Ball & Thomas, Cincinnati, ca. 1860s, Albumen print, carte de visite (from: Willis [1993, *J. P. Ball*], 208).

As Marcy Dinius has argued, media cannot be isolated from each other: "there can be no visual culture without print culture and vice versa." This also challenges narratives of African American literary history that contrast the liberating world of orality and the supposedly limiting world of the image.[26] Key authors like Frederick Douglass and Harriet Jacobs used photography in their self-representation or responded to visual culture in multilayered texts. As Sarah Blackwood shows, they "were sensitive to the dynamic between the truthful and deceptive qualities of the photograph."[27] Following Henry Louis Gates's groundbreaking work, most critics of nineteenth-century African American literature have focused on intertextuality, on "signifying" and hence on verbal expression.[28] The visual turn, however, affects the field more and more. Now critics investigate the inextricable links between verbal and pictorial cultural expression by antebellum African Americans – or, as Michael Chaney puts it, "the way ex-slaves negotiate authority through multimedia representations."[29]

This takes us back to the photographer advertising in 1854 Cincinnati. In the many years of his long career, James Presley Ball, black businessman and artist, portrayed sitters of all ethnic backgrounds: whites, Asian Americans, African Americans. His black subjects, certainly most significant in this context, sat for Ball in dignified poses that commanded respect. They wore elegant dresses, suits, and hats that seemed newly acquired, documenting their middle-class status. Apart from being known as durable, cheap, lifelike, and beautiful, Ball's images open a window on African American life that could not be more different from the racist cartoons circulating at the same time. In 1869 the photographer also portrayed Frederick Douglass, an African American celebrity. But the pictures studying unknown black subjects are particularly interesting. Visual constructions of white middle-class respectability depended on caricaturing African Americans as the cartoonish other. Ball's sophisticated portraits of black consumers thus challenged the cultural hierarchies of their time.

In a 1999 essay, American art historian Colin Westerbeck discounts Ball's oeuvre as comparatively inauthentic. The sitters, Westerbeck proclaims, "typically assumed clichéd poses of gentility found in the daguerreotypes that white operators made of white subjects." He thinks it odd that Ball's black customers "suggest a life of leisure." These subjects, Westerbeck finds, "do not appear to have asserted themselves […] either as African Americans or as individuals."[30] This somewhat sketchy reading of Ball's images seems at odds with larger paradigms in African American cultural history. As Kevin Young's recent *Grey Album* demonstrates, the inauthentic, the counterfeit, and the constructed constitute central forces in black culture. Reading "blackness" as "an improvisatory process," Young discusses the "tradition of reinvention" found in African American expressions.[31] Along similar lines, Daphne Brooks's study of performance history notes that realism may have been too limiting for nineteenth-century "black cultural producers" interested in disrupting the racist narratives of their time.[32]

Seen in this context, Ball's images of genteel black sitters should be read as intricate fictions rather than as failed attempts to realistically portray their protagonists. These photographs document performances. Sitter and photographer, lighting, studio, and props worked together, creating miniature narratives of a black middle class. "The photograph," Wallace and Smith state, "became a key site through which a new identity could be produced and promulgated."[33] Key studies of African American visual culture focus on prominent thinkers and writers – Frederick Douglass, most frequently – and their strategic use of self-portraits in establishing a public persona. However, Douglass himself observed that the "humblest servant girl may now possess a picture of herself such as the wealth of kings could not purchase fifty years ago."[34] James Presley Ball's portraits provided these opportunities. They operated in the sphere of self-presentation rather than in the register of authenticity. In this case, consumption created new aesthetic and cultural forms. Highly skilled in constructing pictorial commodities, Ball enabled African Americans to perform in different terms, on their own terms, in fact, oscillating between black and white identities, ready and able to make use of the codes and fictions of middle-class respectability.

3. Spectacle and Abolitionism: Ball's *Splendid Mammoth Pictorial Tour*

James Presley Ball's case takes us to the nexus of race, image, and text. His photographs reveal new perspectives on African Americans and their self-representations as consumers and citizens. Preserved by photography's archivists, these documents continue to fascinate even twenty-first-century viewers. Ironically, however, the most impressive images

Ball ever produced are lost. In the year 1855, Ball had envisioned a project that was much larger – literally – than his portrait business. He produced an exhibition generously titled *Ball's Splendid Mammoth Pictorial Tour of the United States Comprising Views of the African Slave Trade; of Northern and Southern Cities; of Cotton and Sugar Plantations; of the Mississippi, Ohio and Susquehanna Rivers, Niagara Falls, & c: Compiled for the Panorama*. A monumental production, the collection of artworks extended for 600 yards. It combined paintings by Robert S. Duncanson, an African American landscape artist, and pictures made by Ball himself. 53 images of 53 different places were on display: representations of Africa, the United States, and Canada. Ball's exhibition functioned in the context of visual spectacle. The *Splendid Mammoth Pictorial Tour*, the local attraction of Cincinnati in 1855, made size its key selling point. "2400 square yards of canvas," the curator announced. "This we take it is considerably longer and wider than any other work of the kind."[35]

Oversized paintings, landscapes mostly, ranked as hot consumer items in antebellum America. The artist John Banvard, Ball's contemporary, was said to have made the enormous profit of 200,000 dollars with the presentation of the "Biggest Picture in the World," claimed to be three miles long. Over 400,000 spectators had come to see Banvard's show in New York City, New Orleans, and Washington, D.C. Other painters had followed suit, in various cities, even in Ball's own Cincinnati.[36] And yet, Ball's project didn't just play the size card. It functioned in two discourses at the same time. While partaking in the culture of superlative spectacle, it was also designed as a cultural text in the framework of the "abolitionist imagination."[37] The exhibition showed monumental views of African vegetation, Louisiana bayous, plantation scenes, city squares, and spectacular Niagara Falls. And its narrative arc followed slavery – from the African slave trade to the Middle Passage to slavery in the South, and on to slave uprisings, escapes, the abolitionist movement, the Underground Railroad. Most paintings were landscapes. Others depicted scenes of Middle Passage suffering on ships or of hunters and their dogs pursuing runaway slaves.

Like a few other African American performers and entrepreneurs of his time, Ball mixed the spectacular and the political in order to find an audience. Henry Box Brown, for instance, a man who had escaped from the South hidden in a crate, reenacted his feat repeatedly, combining "publicity stunts" and "abolitionist propaganda" in his public appearances.[38]

As Daphne Brooks notes, such performances rewrote the "ubiquitous master narrative of minstrelsy."[39] Ball's spectacular project used a similar approach. Conjuring up the invisible images of the lost exhibition helps us see even more clearly that nineteenth-century visual culture offered far more than vicious racism. There are good reasons to overcome antebellum iconophobia.

Coming back to the force field of image and text, race and consumer culture, it is even more interesting to explore how Ball used writing and visual material to address both the atrocities of slavery and the everyday lives of free black men and women. While the paintings did not survive, a pamphlet accompanying the show did. Thanks to Deborah Willis, the text is available to twenty-first-century readers: a 56-page book eponymous to the exhibition, published in 1855 by Achilles Pugh, a Cincinnati printer. Its author, most probably James Presley Ball, prefaced the booklet with a modest note. He stated that "[n]o literary excellence" was "claimed," calling his work "a plain attempt to record plain facts for plain people." The author asserted to have "endeavored to avoid the insertion of any thing that cannot be substantiated as truth" (247).

These notes perform familiar gestures. Particularly in slave narratives, to claim authenticity was a standard textual element. And for the most part, the booklet adheres to the codes of the factual and the sober, describing the slavery system based on historical literature, data, and figures. The pamphlet's author demonstrates avid reading on the slavery complex. His essay pulls together a wide variety of sources, most of them from the field of abolitionist writing. It features excerpts by British abolitionist author Thomas Fowell Buxton and John Greenleaf Whittier's poem "The Slave-Ships." Just as visitors were touring the exhibition, gazing at landscapes, cityscapes, and scenes depicting historical events, the text of the pamphlet tours the nineteenth-century knowledge production on the slavery system.

Ball's *Splendid Mammoth Pictorial Tour* operated in the realm of non-fiction – a deceptively simple genre. True stories were important consumer products in antebellum America. This was the era of penny press journalism, a cultural form aiming for the largest possible number of readers by promising nothing but authentic facts. As Peter West argues, the "language of truth," however shaky a concept, was sold to mid-nineteenth-century consumers all over the United States. And new technological developments (the telegraph, an ever more extensive rail system, steam power) helped spread the sensational true stories responsible for the newspaper's commercial success.[40] Beginning in the eighteen-twenties, crime news had become a staple of this new journalism. True stories of the bizarre were expected to appeal to the rapidly growing numbers of working-class readers.[41]

The "plain facts for plain people" (247) in Ball's pamphlet had similar functions. Though sometimes sober and scholarly, the text also veers toward the thrilling and the sentimental. Not unlike a modern-day photographer, the author of the pamphlet selects scenes, passages, fragments that seem particularly spectacular. Taken from the *Utica Morning Herald*, excerpts describing a New Orleans slave auction call up sentimentalism and eroticism in describing the sale of "one of the most beautiful young women [the observer] ever saw [...], her form [...] graceful in the extreme" or the destruction of family bonds between a "noble-looking mulatto women" and her children, one of them a "beautiful bright eyed little boy," one of them sold to Mississippi, the other to Texas (271). Another passage, looking at the other end of the slave trade, quotes from a much earlier account from Africa, of slaves who had not been bought by traders – and left to their own devices:

> Again and again [...] have I seen one or more of these poor creatures, when unable from sickness to walk, crawling on their hands and knees, accompanying the gang to which they are chained, in search of food, for one could not move without the other. In consequence of such treatment they would soon become so emaciated, that the slave dealers would not purchase them on any terms, in which state horrible as it may seem, they were left to perish, without food, medicine or clothing, their bones protruding from their skins, they presented the appearance of living skeletons, lingering amidst hunger and disease and dirt, till death their only friend, released most of them from captivity. (256-257)

Ball's audience in Cincinnati must have associated the horrifying descriptions gleaned from Buxton's 1838 *African Slave Trade* with the photographs they were used to seeing in Ball's gallery: the portraits he had made of whites and African Americans posing in their Sunday best. The camera, a modern apparatus, enabled the sitters to display themselves as middle-class subjects. They documented their freedom to choose – as consumers. Men and women selected J. P. Ball as their photographer, perhaps based on his advertisements. And they selected clothes and props just as they decided on the poses they struck.

To these images of freedom, the pamphlet links the most atrocious evocations of slavery. Intensely contrasting what could be seen on the walls, the pages conjured up Africans treated as commodities, or, to use Agamben's term, as "bare life" – human beings set apart, unclothed, unfed, left to die.[42] It is no accident that "death their only friend" (257) appears as the only individual the passage refers to. As in so many texts on American slaves, these Africans are described as the "permanent subjects of subjection" Michael Chaney has identified in the abolitionist discourse.[43] We could read this critically, arguing in Marcus Wood's terms that nineteenth-century "stylistic giganticism" often "protected audiences from the horror of slavery."[44]

A more flexible reading would explore how the gripping texts and images of James Presley Ball's exhibition operated as elements of a larger project: a heterogeneous narrative moving along the most important fault line running through antebellum American culture. On the one hand, an ever more dynamic consumer society brought forth omnipresent newspapers, advertising, and spectacular entertainment. On the other hand, slavery and representations of slaves supplied fundamentally different concepts of personhood. These concepts were at once utterly alien to a consumer culture and inextricably linked to the circulation of images and goods in the United States. The pamphlet thus touched on two extremes at the same time, portraying Africans and African Americans as both commodities and consumers, emphasizing the enormous distance between these two roles. And yet, this distance could collapse instantly, depending on the given context – especially after the passing of the Fugitive Slave Act.

As critical readers, we could easily discount Ball's pamphlet as a mere collection of quotations, a minor text piecing together bits and pieces from the burgeoning abolitionist discourse. In one passage of Ball's *Splendid Mammoth Pictorial Tour*, however, the pattern breaks up. Cincinnati readers were confronted with an event that was very close in time and space. Something remarkable had taken place "[a] few weeks since," in Cairo, the town located on the confluence of the Ohio and Mississippi rivers. And in this case, the account is first-hand – for once, not based on another contemporary's work. The author, who may have been James Presley Ball, a free black man and businessman, tells the story of another free black entrepreneur, a gentleman named Spencer, who operated a "restaurat [sic] and boarding house" on a boat sitting on the Mississippi river.

Like Ball, the talented photographer, Spencer was highly qualified. According to the text, he "possessed in a high degree that skill in cookery, which some assign as one of the instincts of his race." Hence, he had established himself as a successful businessman: "his boat was largely patronized by the traveling public" (284).

What sounds like a rare and upbeat narrative abruptly shifts direction. The reader learns that Spencer's success "aroused the jealousy of some of the whites in the same line of business." Rivals, cooks, apparently, formed a "combination" to "drive him from the place" (284). From here on, the story of local restaurant competition and race intensifies:

> He [Spencer] was a man devoid of fear, and well suited to defy the horde of wretches by whom he was surrounded. Having been summoned to appear before a magistrate to answer a suit for debt, he attended, carrying a keg of powder under his arm, and a pistol ready to fire into it. The Magistrate afraid of such a dangerous customer, permitted him to depart. The mob assembled that night, determined to destroy his property, and drive him from the place. He received them warmly, firing volley after volley into the crowd, until eleven of them had been shot, three of whom afterwards died. After several hours fighting they boarded the boat, to which they set fire, and towing her into the river, set her adrift. The dauntless Spencer then mounted the roof of the boat, holding in his hand a portion of the stove which he had secured around his neck with a cord. Giving a loud shout of defiance, as the blaze revealed his figure to those on shore, he leapt into the water which closed over him forever. (284)

Again, as in the pamphlet's (or Buxton's) sketch of African horrors, an episode ends with a black subject expecting certain death. Clearly, however, the segment also highlights other facets. The "horde of wretches" here, the anonymous group, many of them killed, does not consist of enslaved blacks, but of white businessmen aiming to shut down their nonwhite rival. The pamphlet evokes a heroic African American individual instead of a group of suffering victims. Spencer, a highly skilled cook and successful entrepreneur, creatively and aggressively designed his end as a spectacular performance. The pamphlet's irony cannot be overlooked. "He received them warmly, firing volley after volley into the crowd": the nonchalance of the phrase is striking.

Moving from evocations of African atrocities to this account of a black businessman's radical self-defense, the pamphlet takes us from slavery's limits of representation to the service economy of the eighteen-fifties. The restaurant, misspelled in the pamphlet, was a comparatively new institution, still rare in the United States and associated with European urban modernity.[45] Catering to numerous customers, Spencer had achieved success in the new service sector. It seems as if his own death had also been enacted to shock the greatest possible number of spectators. After killing and injuring his enemies, he chains himself to a part of his stove, the instrument of his skills and success. It is impossible to ignore the highly performative nature of this suicide. And it is even more obvious that the author of *Ball's Splendid Mammoth Pictorial Tour* found this very impressive. Here, the text opened up options that were closed to Ball's respectable photographs. The writer envisioned excessive violence – a spectacle of weapons, blood and fire provoked by white racism and black retaliation.

4. Conclusion

A nineteenth-century photographer long ignored, James Presley Ball has now turned into the subject of innovative scholarship. Since his rediscovery, a large retrospective exhibition and essays investigating his portraits have emphasized his thoroughly original perspective on the sitters he portrayed. Scholars are fascinated by Ball's images and their representation of dignified, nuanced individuals of all sorts of ethnic backgrounds.[46] And much more could be said about his photographs as cultural texts. They anticipate the ambivalences of modern and postmodern consumer cultures – frameworks that perpetuate racial ideologies and white normativity while offering avenues for minority subjects to achieve equal status and demonstrate the modernity of their lifestyles.[47]

Ball's *Splendid Mammoth Pictorial Tour* remains almost invisible. And this doesn't seem overly baffling. After all, most parts of the ambitious project were destroyed. Moreover, it is certainly difficult to treat the show's one surviving element, the pamphlet published by Achilles Pugh, as a literary text of great complexity and autonomy. The result of a businessman's ambition, it seems too close to the superficialities of consumer culture. Aiming to please, shock, and entertain its readers, it moves around from one titillating quotation to the next, adding a generous dose of J. P. Ball's self-marketing, his career described as an "illustration of the invincible power of energy, and perseverance combined" (249).

And yet, precisely because it possesses these commercial qualities, *Ball's Splendid Mammoth Pictorial Tour* takes us to a crucial historical entanglement. Ball's project responded to a national culture on the brink of war, to a nation constantly debating race, slavery, and human rights in text and image while writers and artists also responded to the pressures of a new consumer culture based on visual spectacle. Race and consumerism were tightly linked, even in the antebellum United States. And these connections call for further research. We know a lot about Melville and Hawthorne, mid-nineteenth-century authors withdrawing from shallow commercialism and heated abolitionism both.[48] We know almost as much about Frederick Douglass's negotiations with race, text, and image, his role as an "observer of and participant in" discussions concerning antebellum photography and egalitarian representation.[49] James Presley Ball's works take us to less familiar territory. We see images and texts designed by a businessman in order to please his customers. Yet apart from being lifelike, beautiful, durable and cheap, Ball's commodities set heterogeneous fragments into motion. Somewhere amid the excerpts describing chained slaves, the daguerreotypes of respectable citizens, and the account of Spencer's skills and rage, antebellum consumers must have begun to grasp the African American experience.

Notes

[1] Marcus Wood (2000). *Blind Memory. Visual Representations of Slavery in England and America, 1780-1865*. Manchester: Manchester University Press, 89.

[2] Qtd. in: Deborah Willis (1993). "Introduction." *J. P. Ball: Daguerrean and Studio Photographer*. Ed. D. W. New York: Garland, xvi (xiii-xix). Further references to this edition will be included in the text.

[3] Recent histories of the relationship between photography and literature insist that to writers, image-makers, and consumers the factuality of the image was not a given at all. As Daniel Novak shows, the manipulation of photographs was "seen not as anomalous or incidental to the project of realism but as absolutely *essential* to it" (4) (emphasis in the text). See also: Armstrong, Nancy (1999). *Fiction in the Age of Photography: The Legacy of British Realism.* Cambridge: Harvard University Press.

[4] Jane M. Rabb (1995). "Introduction." *Literature and Photography: Interactions 1840-1990.* Ed. J. M. R. Albuquerque: University of New Mexico Press, xxxviii (xxxv-lx).

[5] Marcy J. Dinius (2012). *The Camera and the Press: American Visual and Print*

Culture in the Age of the Daguerreotype. Philadelphia: University of Pennsylvania Press, 4.
[6] Miles Orvell (2003). *American Photography*. Oxford: Oxford University Press, 27-28.
[7] Shawn Michelle Smith (1999*). American Archives: Gender, Race, and Class in Visual Culture*. Princeton: Princeton University Press, 13.
[8] Orvell (2003), 28-29.
[9] Smith (1999), 54.
[10] Anon. (1997). "The Literature of Slavery and Freedom." *The Norton Anthology of African American Literature*. Ed. Henry Louis Gates, Jr. and Nellie Y. McKay. New York: Norton, 159 (151-162).
[11] I am drawing on another central literary history here: Eric J. Sundquist (1995). "The Literature of Expansion and Race." *The Cambridge History of American Literature*. Volume Two: Prose Writing, 1820-1865. Ed. Sacvan Bercovitch. Cambridge: Cambridge University Press, 315 (125-328).
[12] "The Literature of Slavery and Freedom" (1997), 151.
[13] John Stauffer (2009). "Douglass's Self-Making and the Culture of Abolitionism." *The Cambridge Companion to Frederick Douglass*. Ed. Maurice S. Lee. Cambridge: Cambridge University Press, 19 (13-30).
[14] Lindon Barrett (1999). *Blackness and Value: Seeing Double*. Cambridge: Cambridge University Press, 217.
[15] Sarah Blackwood (2009). "Fugitive Obscura: Runaway Slave Portraiture and Early Photographic Technology." *American Literature* 81:1, 99 (93-125).
[16] Wood (2000), 87-89.
[17] Daphne A. Brooks (2006). *Bodies in Dissent: Spectacular Performances of Race and Freedom, 1850-1910*. Durham: Duke University Press, 25; Saidiya V. Hartmann (1997). *Scenes of Subjection: Terror, Slavery, and Self-Making in Nineteenth-Century America*. New York: Oxford University Press, 30-32.
[18] See for a fascinating study: Benjamin Reiss (2001). *The Showman and the Slave: Race, Death, and Memory in P.T. Barnum's America*. Cambridge: Harvard University Press.
[19] James C. Davis (2007). *Commerce in Color: Race, Consumer Culture, and American Literature, 1893-1993*. Ann Arbor: University of Michigan Press, 7.
[20] Michael Chaney (2009). *Fugitive Vision: Slave Image and Black Identity in Antebellum Narrative*. Bloomington: Indiana University Press, 6.
[21] Smith (1999), 47.
[22] Wood (2000), 186.
[23] Armstrong (1999), 1.
[24] See her monograph on J. P. Ball as well as her sweeping history of African American photographers: Deborah Willis (2000). *Reflections in Black: A History of Black Photographers 1840 to the Present*. New York: Norton.
[25] Maurice O. Wallace, and Shawn Michelle Smith (2012). "Introduction: Pictures

and Progress." *Pictures and Progress: Early Photography and the Making of African American Identity*. Eds. M. O. W. and S. M. S. Durham: Duke University Press, 4 (1-17).

[26] Dinius (2012), 194, 238.

[27] Blackwood (2009), 95.

[28] *Ibid*., 94.

[29] Chaney (2009), 13.

[30] Colin L. Westerbeck (1999). "Frederick Douglass Chooses His Moment." *Art Institute of Chicago Museum Studies* 24:2, 155 (144-161 and 260-262).

[31] Kevin Young (2012). *The Grey Album: On the Blackness of Blackness*. Minneapolis: Graywolf, 262.

[32] Brooks (2006), 6.

[33] Wallace/Smith (2012), 5.

[34] Qtd. in: *Ibid*., 6.

[35] Anonymously published as (1855) *Ball's Splendid Mammoth Pictorial Tour of the United States Comprising Views of the African Slave Trade; of Northern and Southern Cities; of Cotton and Sugar Plantations; of the Mississippi, Ohio and Susquehanna Rivers, Niagara Falls, & c: Compiled for the Panorama*. Cincinnati: Achilles Pugh. [In: Willis, Deborah (ed.) (1993). *J. P. Ball: Daguerrean and Studio Photographer.* New York: Garland, 243-299.]. Further references will be included in the text.

[36] Theresa Leininger-Miller (2011). "Review: An American Journey: The Life and Photography of James Presley Ball." *Nineteenth-Century Art Worldwide: A Journal of Nineteenth-Century Visual Culture* 10.2, Autumn 2011: n. p. Web. 30 September 2013 <http://www.19thc-artworldwide.org/autumn11/review-of-an-american-journey-the-life-and-photography-of-james-presley-ball>.

[37] Andrew Delbanco (2012). *The Abolitionist Imagination*. Cambridge: Harvard University Press.

[38] Brooks (2006), 66.

[39] *Ibid*., 5.

[40] Peter West (2008). *The Arbiters of Reality: Hawthorne, Melville, and the Rise of Mass Information Culture.* Columbus: Ohio State University Press, 3.

[41] Andie Tucher (1994). *Froth & Scum: Truth, Beauty, Goodness, and the Ax Murder in America's First Mass Medium*. Chapel Hill: University of North Carolina Press, 11-12.

[42] See: Giorgio Agamben (1998). *Homo Sacer: Sovereign Power and Bare Life.* Stanford: Stanford University Press.

[43] Chaney (2009), 6.

[44] Wood (2000), 182.

[45] Waverly Root and Richard de Rochemont (1976). *Eating in America: A History.* Hopewell: Ecco, 313-314.

[46] See Smith's close reading of a series produced by Ball in Montana, images of

an African American hanged in public: Smith, Shawn Michelle (2012). "The Photographer's Touch: J. P. Ball." *Pictures and Progress*. Eds. Maurice O. Wallace and S. M. S. Durham: Duke University Press, 321-328.

47 Davis (2007), 11.

48 See West's and Delbanco's studies, the former taking the literary perspective, the latter exploring Melville and Hawthorne in their political context.

49 Dinius (2012), 194.

Bibliography

Agamben, Giorgio (1998). *Homo Sacer: Sovereign Power and Bare Life*. Stanford: Stanford University Press.

Anon. (1855). *Ball's Splendid Mammoth Pictorial Tour of the United States comprising Views of the African Slave Trade; of Northern and Southern Cities; of Cotton and Sugar Plantations; of the Mississippi, Ohio and Susquehanna Rivers, Niagara Falls, & c: Compiled for the Panorama*. Cincinnati: Achilles Pugh. [In: Willis, Deborah (ed.) (1993). *J. P. Ball: Daguerrean and Studio Photographer*. New York: Garland, 243-299.]

Anon. (1997). "The Literature of Slavery and Freedom." *The Norton Anthology of African American Literature*. Ed. Henry Louis Gates, Jr. and Nellie Y. McKay. New York: Norton, 151-162.

Armstrong, Nancy (1999). *Fiction in the Age of Photography: The Legacy of British Realism*. Cambridge: Harvard University Press.

Barrett, Lindon (1999). *Blackness and Value: Seeing Double*. Cambridge: Cambridge University Press.

Blackwood, Sarah (2009). "Fugitive Obscura: Runaway Slave Portraiture and Early Photographic Technology." *American Literature* 81.1, 93-125.

Brooks, Daphne A. (2006). *Bodies in Dissent: Spectacular Performances of Race and Freedom, 1850-1910*. Durham: Duke University Press.

Chaney, Michael (2009). *Fugitive Vision: Slave Image and Black Identity in Antebellum Narrative*. Bloomington: Indiana University Press.

Davis, James C. (2007). *Commerce in Color: Race, Consumer Culture, and American Literature, 1893-1993*. Ann Arbor: University of Michigan Press.

Delbanco, Andrew (2012). *The Abolitionist Imagination*. Cambridge: Harvard University Press.

Dinius, Marcy J. (2012). *The Camera and the Press: American Visual and Print Culture in the Age of the Daguerreotype*. Philadelphia: University of Pennsylvania Press.

Hartman, Saidiya V. (1997). *Scenes of Subjection: Terror, Slavery, and Self-Making in Nineteenth-Century America*. New York: Oxford University Press.

Leininger-Miller, Theresa (2011). "Review: An American Journey: The Life and Photography of James Presley Ball." *Nineteenth-Century Art Worldwide: A Journal of Nineteenth-Century Visual Culture* 10.2, Autumn 2011: Web. 30 September 2013 <http://www.19thc-artworldwide.org/autumn11/ review-of-an-american-journey-the-life-and-photography-of-james-presley-ball>.

Novak, Daniel A. (2008). *Realism, Photography, and Nineteenth-Century Fiction*. Cambridge: Cambridge University Press.

Orvell, Miles (2003). *American Photography*. Oxford: Oxford University Press.

Rabb, Jane M. (1995). "Introduction." *Literature and Photography: Interactions 1840-1990*. Ed. J. M. R. Albuquerque: University of New Mexico Press, xxxv-lx.

Reiss, Benjamin (2001). *The Showman and the Slave: Race, Death, and Memory in P. T. Barnum's America*. Cambridge: Harvard University Press.

Root, Waverly, and Richard de Rochemont (1976). *Eating in America: A History*. Hopewell: Ecco.

Smith, Shawn Michelle (1999). *American Archives: Gender, Race, and Class in Visual Culture*. Princeton: Princeton University Press.

--- (2012). "The Photographer's Touch: J. P. Ball." *Pictures and Progress: Early Photography and the Making of African American Identity*. Eds. Maurice O. Wallace and S. M. S. Durham: Duke University Press, 321-328.

Stauffer, John (2009). "Douglass's Self-Making and the Culture of Abolitionism." *The Cambridge Companion to Frederick Douglass*. Ed. Maurice S. Lee. Cambridge: Cambridge University Press, 13-30.

Sundquist, Eric J. (1995). "The Literature of Expansion and Race." *The Cambridge History of American Literature.* Vol. 2: Prose Writing, 1820-1865. Ed. Sacvan Bercovitch. Cambridge: Cambridge University Press, 125-328.

Tucher, Andie (1994). *Froth & Scum: Truth, Beauty, Goodness, and the Ax Murder in America's First Mass Medium*. Chapel Hill: University of North Carolina Press.

Wallace, Maurice O., and Shawn Michelle Smith (2012). "Introduction." *Pictures and Progress: Early Photography and the Making of African American Identity*. Eds. M. O. W. and S. M. S. Durham: Duke University Press, 1-17.

West, Peter (2008). *The Arbiters of Reality: Hawthorne, Melville, and the Rise of Mass Information Culture*. Columbus: Ohio State University Press.

Westerbeck, Colin (1999). "Frederick Douglass Chooses His Moment." *Art Institute of Chicago Museum Studies* 24.2, 144-161 and 260-262.

Willis, Deborah (1993). "Introduction." *J. P. Ball: Daguerrean and Studio Photographer*. Ed. D. W. New York: Garland, xiii-xix.

--- (ed.) (1993). *J. P. Ball: Daguerrean and Studio Photographer*. New York: Garland.

--- (2000). *Reflections in Black: A History of Black Photographers, 1840 to the Present*. New York: Norton.

Wood, Marcus (2000). *Blind Memory: Visual Representations of Slavery in England and America, 1780-1865*. Manchester: Manchester University Press.
Young, Kevin (2012). *The Grey Album: On the Blackness of Blackness*. Minneapolis: Graywolf.

Klara Stephanie Szlezák (Regensburg)

Sages and Souvenirs: The Origins of American Literary Tourism in Concord, Massachusetts

1. Literature and Consumption

Literature and consumption touch upon each other in numerous ways. Texts are consumed – and 'digested' – in the very act of reading. To a considerable degree, the production of literature either takes shape according to or finds itself in conflict with the book market, which is, just like any other market, subject to a balancing of supply and demand. Consumption not only relates to literature in the sense that books can be bought and read, but in the sense that it is turned into a literary theme in its own right.

In the nineteenth-century United States, the curtain for important developments in the book market was drawn. A national market emerged and consumption as a cultural phenomenon reached unprecedented dimensions. Debates over authorship as a pastime or a profession ignited and spread in the first decades of the nineteenth century. Writers such as Washington Irving and James Fenimore Cooper, taking their cues from conditions in Great Britain, were among the first to defend authorship against accusations of idleness and lack of common benefit. Henry Wadsworth Longfellow vehemently argued for the manliness and usefulness of poetry in his 1832 pamphlet "Defence of Poetry." Nathaniel Hawthorne still saw the need to counter the stigma and to argue for the legitimacy of authorship in his 1850 essay "The Custom-House," prefacing his novel *The Scarlet Letter*.

Concomitantly with ideological struggles, technical and economic conditions evolved that changed literature's role in American society. Improved techniques of paper production and printing secured affordability, while the expansion of the railroad promised wider availability. Increased literacy through improved schooling augmented the readership. Furthermore, the rise of magazine culture was to change the image and circulation of fictional writing, retrieving the American novel from the depths of disrepute.[1]

These developments and discourses closely relate to a phenomenon that establishes a connection between literature and consumption in yet another way: literary tourism, simply defined as "tourism activity that is motivated by interest in an author, a literary creation or setting, or the literary heritage of a destination."[2] Literary tourism provides a further way for readers and/as travelers to consume literature.

The goal of this article is to trace the development of literary tourism in the United States in the nineteenth century and to explore the diverse driving forces that turned Concord, Massachusetts, into a 'literary mecca' and one of the nation's foremost destinations for literary tourists. Historical circumstances, geographical conditions, and conscious efforts to promote Concord concerted to lay the foundations of the town's successful history as a, if not *the*, major point of attraction for American literary tourism.

2. Literary Tourism in the Nineteenth-Century United States

In his 1841 essay "Self-Reliance," Concord's almost proverbial 'sage' Ralph Waldo Emerson proclaimed: "It is for want of self-culture that the superstition of Travelling, whose idols are Italy, England, Egypt, retains its fascination for all educated Americans."[3] Emerson's comment on the American mid-century "superstition" to travel abroad matters in the present context for two reasons. First, Emerson explicitly links travel to education (and thus implicitly to class). It was a wide-spread belief that the interest in traveling and visiting places away from home sprang from a certain level of education, as did the capacity to appreciate and comprehend the things and people that Americans encountered on their travels. Second, Emerson puts the fashion of traveling abroad down to "the want of self-culture" in the mid-nineteenth-century United States. Both factors have an impact on the development of literary tourism.

The link between travel and education was crucial for the rise of literary tourism in the United States. Generally, travel at the time was less motivated by a desire for leisure than by a desire for further education. And the desire to set off and visit the birthplaces, homes, or graves of authors like Emerson, Hawthorne, Irving, Longfellow, Thoreau and others was predominantly felt by those who had access to an education that allowed them to be familiar with these authors' writings. Literary tourism was set in a larger context of developments in nineteenth-century American tourism that directed interest toward stateside travel. In her book *See America First*, Marguerite Shaffer argues that "tourism emerged as a form of geographical consumption that centered on the sights and scenes of the American nation." To Shaffer, tourism "was integrally connected to the emergence of the United States as a corporate urban-industrial nation-state."[4] Emerson's observation of the "want of self-culture"[5] came at a point in time when the country's own culture was just being discovered and progressively appropriated for tourism – literary sites included.

If American tourists increasingly turned to domestic sites, the inspiration for their peregrinations did come from abroad. While the practice of literary tourism reaches back to ancient times, it was in nineteenth-century Great Britain that some of its defining characteristics took shape. Harald Hendrix describes its evolution as the development from

> the gradually evolving relationship between readers, authors and texts on the one hand, to the appropriation of essentially elitist and universalist habits into emergent mass cultures susceptible of supporting nationalist ideologies on the other.[6]

Poets' Corner in Westminster Abbey, Shakespeare's Stratford-upon-Avon, Wordsworth's Dove Cottage, and Sir Walter Scott's Abbotsford were just some of the destinations that attracted many American tourists. Those who could not come to see these landmarks for themselves were familiar with them through the increasing number of travel accounts.[7] In fact, the popularity of the British itinerary was unsurpassed for the larger part of the nineteenth century. According to Paul Westover, for "an America of interest to literary tourists" to emerge, "a literary America" had to crystallize first.[8]

When literary tourism evolved in the nineteenth-century United States, it did so, not surprisingly, around the centers of literary culture at the time: in the Northeast. Published in 1853, the illustrated volume *Homes of American Authors, Comprising Anecdotical, Personal, and Descriptive Sketches* appears to be the first book publication dedicated to American writers' houses. It provides glimpses into the homes of seventeen authors, including Irving, William Cullen Bryant, Richard Henry

Dana, Catharine Maria Sedgwick, Emerson, Hawthorne, and James Russell Lowell. The majority of these residences were located in New England. Indeed, the American writers in whose homes the public was thought to be interested were "too numerous to be all included in one volume,"[9] necessitating the planning of a second volume.[10] While this book, and many others in its wake, mirrored and responded to the public's interest in the authors and their daily lives, the professional operation of writers' houses as museums did not set in until the turn of the century. John Greenleaf Whittier's birthplace in Haverhill and his home in Amesbury, Massachusetts were both preserved and made accessible to the public in the eighteen-nineties. Other sites which came to be professionally organized at an early point in time were Longfellow's birthplace in Portland, Maine, in 1901, and the Alcotts' Orchard House in Concord in 1911. While the musealization of writers' houses took place in the wider context of the colonial revival and the historic preservation movement, literary tourism as a form of consumption evolved before the turn of the century.

As identified by Mike Robinson and Hans Christian Andersen, the defining features of literary tourism include the "consumption, production, re-production, commodification, transformation, communication, and distribution of literature for tourism purposes."[11] The case of Concord shows that literary tourism also links the consumption of literature to the consumption of place. Access to literature is supposed to be gained through the experience of place; a fictionalized environment or a site closely related to a writer's biography. John Urry points out that places have traditionally been neglected in the study of consumption and have not been accorded the consideration and discussion they deserve. Urry ranks sites next to "things," consumer goods and objects, and convincingly argues that they can be consumed quite literally but also visually. "Places are chosen to be gazed upon," Urry writes, "because there is an anticipation [...] of intense pleasures," an anticipation which is consciously "constructed and sustained."[12] The continuing existence of a sense of anticipation associated with a site will guarantee the consumers' interest. Concord was the one place in the United States in which literary tourism emerged and thrived particularly visibly in the nineteenth century and which was thus consumed on a (comparatively) large scale.

3. Concord's Rise as America's 'Literary Mecca'

In his book *The American Scene*, published in 1907, Henry James dedicated one chapter to Concord and Salem in Massachusetts. He coined one of the most widely known descriptions of Concord when he called it "the biggest little place in America," which the country was "lucky to have."[13] His appraisal of Concord rings true in the context of American literary tourism. Concord's "weight," its "character," its "intensity of presence and sweetness of tone," its "moral charm," as well as its "pleasant appreciability," to quote James's catalogue of attributes,[14] partly stemmed from historical circumstances, partly from conscious construction.

The development of Concord into the center of American literary tourism was assisted by at least three major factors. First, there was the town's geographic location and accessibility for visitors. While largely depicted as a pastoral retreat set in an agrarian context, Concord was less of a village than a suburb to Boston. When Concord was connected to the railroad in 1844, the distance was reduced to an hour's train ride.[15] Second, when literary tourism emerged in Concord, the town had already been opened up for sightseers. In 1837, the Concord citizens dedicated the battle monument, which was preceded by heated debates over what place in Concord would be best suited for visitors to commemorate the Revolutionary War battles of Concord and Lexington. The obelisk and the famous old North Bridge attracted visitors, who came to venerate the town's and the nation's patriotic past.[16]

After the Civil War, interest in American history was more pronounced than ever, particularly middle-class interest in a mythical American past that ignored recent shifts and changes in society, such as economic instabilities and a growing ethnic and cultural diversity.[17] Concord was certainly an apt place for such projections. It was widely, if inaccurately, perceived as unaffected by upheavals and heterogeneity. As such it lent itself easily to being adopted into tourism narratives. The town's "profound identification with its past made tourism a local industry as the popularity of historic 'pilgrimages' grew" in the second half of the nineteenth century.[18] Finally, Concord in the mid-nineteenth century was the location of what can be called "a genius cluster."[19] A large number of intellectuals and writers came together in the small community, most of them in response to Emerson relocating there in 1835. In 1936, Van Wyck Brooks published a pictorially written and somewhat clichéd account of the *Flowering of New England*. In his book, Brooks compared these authors to "moths attracted by the [...] Emersonian beacon."[20] Among them, only Thoreau was a Concord native. The town soon came to be perceived as a gathering place for what Franklin Sanborn in the late nineteenth century called "exceptional, imported persons."[21]

Starting from these conditions – accessibility, existing tourism, and the presence of famed writers –, literary tourism in Concord was fuelled by a confluence of efforts that made the consumption of this 'literary mecca' possible. When the number of people who knocked on the Alcotts' and on Emerson's front doors increased and asked to be shown their studies or meet the writers, the potential of Concord as a destination for literary tourism manifested itself. The town and its writers were increasingly commodified. Three phenomena can be singled out which simultaneously were manifestations of and a further stimulus for literary tourism in Concord: promotional texts, visualization, and souvenir business. All three sprang up due to the existence of sites to (re)present and to advertise, and at the same time contributed significantly to the creation and corroboration of sites.

As Robert Gross states, the Concord writers themselves had depicted their town as the "charming fairyland,"[22] an image which can be found in later descriptions. The number of magazine contributions and tourist guide books dedicated to Concord abounded.[23] As a textual genre they were meant both to attract visitors to the actual sites and to make Concord and its writers consumable from afar. An early article on New England writers' houses, "The Homes of America: Some New England Houses III," published in *The Art Journal* in 1878, describes the multifaceted attractiveness of Concord. It presents a rural idyll fostering thought and creativity:

> An hour's ride by rail from Boston brings one to Concord, which enjoys a triple fame; that of having been one of the spots where the first collision took place between the British and the Revolutionary patriots, the home of a remarkable group of philosophers and men of letters, and one of the prettiest and most attractive towns in New England. Its repose, its shaded streets, its neat old-time houses, here and there varied by newer and more showy buildings, its placid winding little river, fringed by meadow, turf, and shrubbery, its sunny fields, its trim but unambitious gardens have a charm of their own, apart from the distinction it has received from the doughty struggle of '75, and the fact that it has been the home of geniuses

> like Hawthorne, Emerson, and Thoreau. No spot or neighborhood, indeed, could be found more congenial to the reverie of the philosopher, or the tranquil travail of the imaginative writer.[24]

The presence, or memory, of "a remarkable group of philosophers and men of letters" is identified as both a result and a source of the appeal of Concord, for these literary men and for the (literary) tourists who trace them. Writing in 1895, Theodore F. Wolfe, in his book *Literary Shrines: The Haunts of Some Famous American Authors*, clearly shifts the focus of local tourism away from Concord's role in the Revolutionary War when he claims that the town drew

> more pilgrims than any other place of equal size upon the continent, not because it holds an historic battle-field, but because it has been the dwelling-place of some of the brightest and best in American letters, who have here written their books and warred against creeds, forms, and intellectual servitude. It is another Stratford, another Mecca, to which come reverent pilgrims from the Old World and the New to worship at its shrines and to wander through the scenes hallowed by the memories of its illustrious *littérateurs*, seers, and evangels.[25]

At the very end of the nineteenth century, Wolfe derives Concord's attractiveness for visitors and tourists more explicitly from the fact that it was the home to "the brightest and best in American letters," claiming for the Concord group not only local or regional, but national significance. By that time, "[a]mong all American places made famous by literary associations, Concord had already long been and still remains today the most visited and the most luminous with the sense of the sacred."[26]

As observable from Theodore Wolfe's – and other authors' – choice of religious vocabulary and as analyzed by Lawrence Buell in his seminal 1989 article "The Thoreauvian Pilgrimage: The Structure of an American Cult," the phenomenon of literary tourism has frequently been cast in the terms of pilgrimage and sacred travel. Setting the focus on Thoreau's Walden and building on the theory of Christian pilgrimage by Victor and Edith Turner,[27] Buell reveals the overlaps between Christian and literary pilgrimages as manifest in the temporary release from the everyday social structures and the "spiritual renewal" made possible through the encounter with and experience of sacred symbols.[28] For the sacralization of Concord to succeed, three fundamental factors fell into place, i.e., the presence of sacred symbols in the form of literary sites or "shrines," their veneration through literary tourists or "pilgrims," and the establishment of a supporting industry. As Ian Ousby has pointed out,

> [p]ilgrims, by definition, trod a beaten path toward a communally agreed, indeed a well-publicised, goal. […] The sale of indulgences – like the trade in minor, portable relics, a common target of attack by reformers – is a powerful reminder of the commercial aspect of the medieval pilgrimage.[29]

Publicity and commerce as essential ingredients of both traditional pilgrimage and literary tourism did not prove incompatible with the "profound spiritual need"[30] which instigated these travels.

Whereas Wolfe's book had also taken into consideration 'literary shrines' outside of Concord, George Tolman's book *Concord: A Few Things to Be Seen There*, published in 1902, is entirely dedicated to the town and grants "the marvelous literary atmosphere that has attained here in years past" preeminence over "the historic battlefield."[31] While it is hard to make the process of literary production visible for readers and visitors, texts like Wolfe's and Tolman's root the invisible in the material world. Concord's inspiring scenery and the sites associated with the writers shall grant the readers and/as visitors insight into where and how literature was written. This rhetoric survived well into the early decades of the twentieth century.

Perry Walton's book *Concord: A Pilgrimage to the Historic and Literary Center of America*, for instance, which appeared in 1922, re-affirms the purpose of previous publications, i.e., "to help the visitor to view Concord with a 'seeing eye' […] and also to understand something of the character of Emerson, Hawthorne, Thoreau, Alcott, and those other rare spirits that have given so much to the world."[32] Walton's observation underscores John Urry's finding that places are extensively consumed through visualization. The book promises that "[i]n the homes of these writers many visitors to Concord find a background into which to fit the authors they love, and gain here an appreciation of the individual behind the book."[33]

Decades before poststructuralist proclamations of the irrelevance of the person of the writer for the reading and understanding of texts – most famously phrased in Roland Barthes's declaration of the "death of the author" –, the "individual behind the book" was unchallenged in his/her authority over the literary texts he/she had produced. Thus these individual biographies proved crucial assets for literary tourism and the construction of literary sites as tourist destinations. In the context of literary tourism, the authority of the "individual behind the book" has been largely unaffected by twentieth-century critical attacks, revealing a wide gap between critical textual analysis and the practice of literary tourism. For sightseers, the individual author remains seminal to this day.

These are just some examples of early publications that bring Concord into the readers' homes and ideally also bring the readers to Concord eventually. The texts share stylistic features that make the Massachusetts town appear close and graspable for experience, such as minute detail in the descriptions of sites or a high frequency of deictic pronouns and adverbs implying proximity. Reading these texts allows us to form mental images of the writers in the streets and in their homes. They aim at creating mental images of Concord and its literary past in the present, as well as the sense of anticipation which fosters tourism.

The creation of mental images was soon supplemented by different forms of actual visualization, which equally testified to Concord's touristic value and made its literary sites accessible to far-off consumers. In the nineteenth century those were primarily book illustrations, in the form of engravings or etchings, and increasingly stereographs and picture postcards. A popular source of home entertainment, the stereograph soon came to occupy a secure place in middle- and upper-class parlors, and pictures of Concord writers' houses counted among the motifs of the 'American scenery.' While most of them show the exterior of the houses, some grant the viewers a glimpse at the interior. The stereographic views of the interior spaces almost exclusively present the writers' studies or libraries, seemingly providing (metaphoric and literal) 'insider' knowledge of the conditions under which some of the nation's foremost literary works were produced.

Many early picture postcards use a particular aesthetic technique to underscore the link between tourist site and writer (see figs. 1 and 2). In addition to the front views of the houses, the postcards show the portrait of the authors, visually associating place and person. In many cases, this combination is further complemented by a well-known quote from the writers' works, often in the nostalgic design of an unrolling parchment. Author, work, and home form a triad of meaning.

Early picture postcard of Emerson's Concord home (Courtesy, American Antiquarian Society).

Early picture postcard of Louisa May Alcott's Concord home (Courtesy, American Antiquarian Society).

While in such postcards literature is explicitly visualized in the picture through actual words from the writings, postcards that show only house and person use both elements to metonymically evoke the literature produced by the writer in the house. In those cases in which the postcards do not place the writer in his or her immediate domestic context tourist sites are actively created, such as the site related to Thoreau's stay at Walden Pond or the Authors' Ridge at the Sleepy Hollow cemetery, opened in 1855.

Postcards occupy the middle ground between advertisement and souvenirs, depending on whether they are sent to someone else, in whom then a sense of anticipation is created, turning them into prospective tourists, or whether they are included in the buyer's collection as keepsakes. Souvenirs, according to Susan Stewart, derive their value from the material relation to their location of origin. The desire for them stems from the fact that the events of which they are reminiscent are not "repeatable;" they are, however, "reportable" so that "through narrative the souvenir substitutes a context of perpetual consumption for its context of origin."[34] The very pamphlets about Concord which tourists used to guide their visit and which originally served as sources of information may have functioned as "souvenirs that visitors kept of their journey," as Ronald A. Bosco suggests.[35]The establishment of a souvenir business drawing on the town's literary tradition was a necessary step for the consolidation of literary tourism at Concord. The photograph below attests to the early awareness of how profitable the literary past was for the local tourism industry (see fig. 3).

Taken at the turn of the century by an unknown photographer, the picture shows the souvenir shop of Edith Buck, who in the eighteen-nineties sold Concord souvenirs out of her little stand at the foot of the drive at The Old Manse, the former home of Emerson and Hawthorne, by the North Bridge. The object file in the Concord Museum identifies the booth as "a very early instance of the marketing of Thoreau's legacy." The file specifies that in 1897, "Thoreau souvenirs outsold those of Emerson and Hawthorne." Among the items which Buck offered to tourists were also fans with views of the North Bridge, the Emerson House, and other area attractions, printed in Boston and decorated and assembled in Japan.

The sign above the shop advertises Emerson and Thoreau souvenirs in large letters. The window display shows a selection of postcard motifs. Small items are presented in two glass cases in front of and to the right of

The Little Shop by the Side of the Road, Concord (Courtesy, Concord Museum, Concord, Massachusetts, USA).

the booth. Additional signs advertise home-made candy, drinks, and cigars. Thus, the photograph also presents the ways in which an emerging tourist industry aimed to satisfy needs among the visitors that were no longer related to literature as the original incentive for the visit. While avid readers of Emerson were easily turned into consumers of Emerson souvenirs, they may concomitantly have turned into buyers of cool drinks, cigars, and candy. Conveniently located by the side of the road and offering mementoes associated with the literary icons of Concord, the stand is both reminiscent of the road side commerce that accompanied medieval pilgrimages and evocative of the ever-growing consumer culture of turn-of-the-century America.[36]

4. Conclusion

In the introduction to his study of American consumer culture from the years 1880 through 1920, Simon Bronner links "the cultural web of consumption"[37] not only to economic conditions but to the emergence and spread of American mass culture. He argues that the significant progress in the realms of communication, transportation, and education was meant to respond and did respond to the exigencies of a growing consumer culture, which altered the face of American business quantitatively and qualitatively.[38] These observations also apply to the historical growth of literary tourism in Concord in this period.

Literary tourism in Concord was initiated by spontaneous visits by devotees of the Concord writers during their lifetimes. It quickly developed into an ever-increasing phenomenon, which was consolidated throughout the twentieth century. It is thus fair to say that Concord sold and sells well. The town was continuously commodified as the cradle of American literary culture through textual and visual representations and memorabilia. This encouraged the unbroken flow of tourists coming into Concord in search of an encounter with some of America's canonical writers. Before the onset of automobile traffic in the twentieth century, the only fast access to Concord was provided by the railroad, and literary tourism relied proportionally more on regional tourists. From the distance, the literary sites of Concord could be predominantly consumed in a mediated form, through guide book accounts and visualizations.

With the introduction of affordable automobiles and the extension of the road system visitor numbers increased and the sites were adapted to this change. Thus, literary tourism in Concord has managed to attract visitors for more than a century. One reason may certainly be that Concord offers its literary tourists a wide spectrum of attractions. They are promised access to the literature written in town via the biographies of the writers, as displayed in the house museums, and via (semi-)fictionalized places, such as Walden Pond, Louisa May Alcott's Orchard House, or Hawthorne's Old Manse. These sites draw their appeal from the middle ground that they occupy, between writer's biography and fiction – an appeal that has been consciously reinforced to cater to a tourist audience. The twenty-first century witnesses the translation of these efforts into the virtual realm. Numerous websites rich in stories and pictures continue to advertise Concord as a unique place promising literary tourists an encounter with nineteenth-century sages that, just like the town itself, have not lost their market value.

Notes

[1] For a detailed survey of the development of the American book market between 1840 and 1880, see: Scott E. Casper, Jeffrey D. Groves, Stephen W. Nissenbaum, and Michael Winship (eds.) (2007). *A History of the Book in America*. Vol. 3. Chapel Hill: University of North Carolina Press, in particular Scott E. Casper's "Introduction."
[2] Melanie Smith, Nicola MacLeod and Margaret Hart Robertson (2010). *Key Concepts in Tourist Studies*. London: Sage, 108.
[3] Ralph Waldo Emerson (2001 [1841]). "Self-Reliance." *Emerson's Prose and Poetry*. Selected and edited by Joel Porte and Saundra Morris. New York: Norton, 133.
[4] Marguerite S. Shaffer (2001). *See America First: Tourism and Identity, 1880-1940*. Washington: Smithsonian Institution Press, 3-4.
[5] Emerson (2001 [1841]), 133.
[6]Harald Hendrix (2009). "From Early Modern to Romantic Tourism: A Diachronical Perspective." *Literary Tourism and Nineteenth-Century Culture*. Ed. Nicola J. Watson. London: Palgrave Macmillan, 13 (13-24).
[7] Paul Westover (2009). "How America 'Inherited' Literary Tourism." *Literary Tourism and Nineteenth-Century Culture*. Ed. Nicola J. Watson. London: Palgrave Macmillan, 185 (184-195).
[8] *Ibid*., 191.
[9] *Homes of American Authors: Comprising Anecdotical, Personal, and Descriptive Sketches, by Various Writers* (1853). New York: Putnam, v.
[10] *Ibid*., vi.
[11] Mike Robinson and Hans Christian Andersen (2002). "Reading Between the Lines: Literature and the Creation of Touristic Spaces." *Literature and Tourism*. Eds. M. R. and H. C. A. London: Continuum, 2 (1-38).
[12] John Urry (1995). *Consuming Places*. London: Routledge, 132.
[13] Henry James (1968 [1907]). *The American Scene*. Bloomington: Indiana University Press, 256.
[14] *Ibid*.
[15] Maura D'Amore (2009). "Thoreau's Unreal Estate: Playing House at Walden Pond." *The New England Quarterly* 82.1, 61 (56-79).
[16] See Robert A. Gross (1999). "The Celestial Village: Transcendentalism and Tourism in Concord." *Transient and Permanent: The Transcendentalist Movement and Its Contexts*. Eds. Charles Chapper and Conrad Edick Wright. Boston: Massachusetts Historical Society, 251-281.
[17] Patricia West (1999). *Domesticating History: The Political Origins of America's House Museums*. Washington: Smithsonian, 42.
[18] *Ibid*., 55. In *Domesticating History*, Patricia West dedicates one chapter to the socio-political circumstances, and in particular to the gender-political contexts,

which turned Louisa May Alcott's former house into a museum; see West (1999), 39-91.

[19] See Susan Cheever (2006). *American Bloomsbury: Louisa May Alcott, Ralph Waldo Emerson, Margaret Fuller, Nathaniel Hawthorne, and Henry David Thoreau: Their Lives, Their Loves, Their Work.* New York: Simon & Schuster, 5.

[20] Van Wyck Brooks (1952 [1936]). *The Flowering of New England, 1815-1865.* New York: The Modern Library, 288. A more recent text which traces the coming-together of those 'geniuses' in Concord is Samuel A. Schreiner's 2006 book *The Concord Quartet*, narrating rather than scholarly investigating "that unique and influential friendship [between Emerson, Amos Bronson Alcott, Thoreau, and Hawthorne] in action, [...] the lives the friends led, and their work that resulted in an enduring change in their nation's direction" (2).

[21] Brooks (1952 [1936]), 64. Another, if minor, factor that made both Concord and its writers visible, and consumable, on a larger, supra-local scale was the lyceum movement of the nineteenth century, which both drew visitors to the Concord lyceum for lectures and which brought Concord writers, most prominently Emerson, for lectures onto different stages outside of Concord and thus contributed to their 'celebrity' status; for a detailed study of the nineteenth-century lyceums in the United States, see Angela G. Ray (2005). *The Lyceum and Public Culture in the Nineteenth-Century United States.* East Lansing: Michigan State University Press.

[22] Gross (1999), 254.

[23] For a survey of early pamphlets and guide books about Concord, see Ronald A. Bosco (2010). "Concord." *The Oxford Handbook of Transcendentalism.* Eds. Joel Myerson, Sandra Harbert Petrulionis, and Laura Dassow Walls. Oxford: Oxford University Press, 477-494.

[24] Anon. (1878). "The Homes of America: Some New England Houses III." *The Art Journal* 4, 164 (161-165).

[25] Theodore F. Wolfe (1895). *Literary Shrines: The Haunts of Some Famous American Authors.* 2nd ed. Philadelphia: Lippincott, 17-18.

[26] Lawrence Buell (1989). "The Thoreauvian Pilgrimage: The Structure of an American Cult." *American Literature* 61.2, 178-179 (175-199).

[27] Victor Turner and Edith Turner (1978). *Image and Pilgrimage in Christian Culture.* New York: Columbia University Press.

[28] Buell (1989), 179.

[29] Ian Ousby (2002 [1990]). *The Englishman's England: Taste, Travel and the Rise of Tourism.* London: Pimlico, 8.

[30] *Ibid.*

[31] George Tolman (1902). *Concord: A Few Things to Be Seen There.* Concord, MA: Patriot Press, 3.

[32] Perry Walton (ed.) (1922). *Concord: A Pilgrimage to the Historic and Literary Center of America.* Boston: Perry Walton, 5.

[33] *Ibid.*, 11.
[34] Susan Stewart (1993). *On Longing: Narratives of the Miniature, the Gigantic, the Souvenir, the Collection*. Durham: Duke University Press, 135.
[35] Bosco (2010), 485.
[36] I am indebted to Adrienne S. Donohue, registrar and collections manager at the Concord Museum, for sharing the contents of the object file with me and answering my questions concerning the souvenir booth. The photograph was published by a Mrs. G. N. Tanner in the early twentieth century, but nothing more is yet known about the circumstances of the publication.
[37] Simon J. Bronner (1989). "Introduction." *Consuming Visions: Accumulation and Display of Goods in America 1880-1920*. Ed. S. J. B. New York: Norton, 1 (1-11).
[38] *Ibid.*

Bibliography

Anon. (1878). "The Homes of America: Some New England Houses III." *The Art Journal* 4, 161-165.

Anon. (1853). *Homes of American Authors: Comprising Anecdotical, Personal, and Descriptive Sketches*. New York: Putnam.

Bosco, Ronald A. (2010). "Concord." *The Oxford Handbook of Transcendentalism*. Eds. Joel Myerson, Sandra Harbert Petrulionis, and Laura Dassow Walls. Oxford: Oxford University Press, 477-494.

Bronner, Simon J. (1989). "Introduction." *Consuming Visions: Accumulation and Display of Goods in America 1880-1920*. Ed. S. J. B. New York: Norton, 1-11.

Brooks, Van Wyck (1952 [1936]). *The Flowering of New England, 1815-1865*. New York: The Modern Library.

Buell, Lawrence (1989). "The Thoreauvian Pilgrimage: The Structure of an American Cult." *American Literature* 61.2, 175-199.

Casper, Scott E. (2007). "Introduction." *A History of the Book in America*. Vol. 3. Eds. Scott E. Casper et al. Chapel Hill: University of North Carolina Press, 1-39.

Casper, Scott E., Jeffrey D. Groves, Stephen W. Nissenbaum, and Michael Winship (eds.) (2007). *A History of the Book in America*. Vol. 3. Chapel Hill: University of North Carolina Press.

Cheever, Susan (2006). *American Bloomsbury: Louisa May Alcott, Ralph Waldo Emerson, Margaret Fuller, Nathaniel Hawthorne, and Henry David Thoreau: Their Lives, Their Loves, Their Work*. New York: Simon & Schuster.

D'Amore, Maura (2009). "Thoreau's Unreal Estate: Playing House at Walden Pond." *The New England Quarterly* 82.1, 56-79.

Emerson, Ralph Waldo (2001 [1841]). "Self-Reliance." *Emerson's Prose and Poetry*. Selected and edited by Joel Porte and Saundra Morris. New York: Norton, 120-137.

Gross, Robert A. (1999). "The Celestial Village: Transcendentalism and Tourism in Concord." *Transient and Permanent: The Transcendentalist Movement and Its Contexts*. Eds. Charles Chapper and Conrad Edick Wright. Boston: Massachusetts Historical Society, 251-281.

Hendrix, Harald (2009). "From Early Modern to Romantic Tourism: A Diachronical Perspective." *Literary Tourism and Nineteenth-Century Culture*. Ed. Nicola J. Watson. London: Palgrave Macmillan, 13-24.

James, Henry (1968 [1907]). *The American Scene*. Bloomington: Indiana University Press.

Ousby, Ian (2002 [1990]). *The Englishman's England: Taste, Travel and the Rise of Tourism*. London: Pimlico.

Ray, Angela G. (2005). *The Lyceum and Public Culture in the Nineteenth-Century United States*. East Lansing: Michigan State University Press.

Robinson, Mike, and Hans Christian Andersen (2002). "Reading Between the Lines: Literature and the Creation of Touristic Spaces." *Literature and Tourism*. Eds. M. R. and H. C. A. London: Continuum, 1-38.

Sanborn, F. B. (1883). *Henry D. Thoreau*. Boston: Houghton Mifflin.

Schreiner, Samuel A. Jr. (2006). *The Concord Quartet: Alcott, Emerson, Hawthorne, Thoreau, and the Friendship That Freed the American Mind*. Hoboken, NJ: Wiley.

Shaffer, Marguerite S. (2001). *See America First: Tourism and Identity, 1880-1940*. Washington: Smithsonian Institution Press.

Smith, Melanie, Nicola MacLeod, and Margaret Hart Robertson (2010). *Key Concepts in Tourist Studies*. London: Sage.

Stewart, Susan (1993). *On Longing: Narratives of the Miniature, the Gigantic, the Souvenir, the Collection*. Durham: Duke University Press.

Tolman, George (1902). *Concord: A Few Things to Be Seen There*. Concord, MA: Patriot Press.

Turner, Victor, and Edith Turner (1978). *Image and Pilgrimage in Christian Culture*. New York: Columbia University Press.

Urry, John (1995). *Consuming Places*. London: Routledge.

Walton, Perry (ed.) (1922). *Concord: A Pilgrimage to the Historic and Literary Center of America*. Boston: Perry Walton.

West, Patricia (1999). *Domesticating History: The Political Origins of America's House Museums*. Washington: Smithsonian.

Westover, Paul (2009). "How America 'Inherited' Literary Tourism." *Literary*

Tourism and Nineteenth-Century Culture. Ed. Nicola J. Watson. London: Palgrave Macmillan, 184-195.

Wolfe, Theodore F. (1895). *Literary Shrines: The Haunts of Some Famous American Authors*. 2nd ed. Philadelphia: Lippincott.

Arthur F. Redding (York University, Toronto)

American Tourism and the Emergence of Mass Culture: Mark Twain's *The Innocents Abroad*

> Then, when I got engaged, [...] my fiancée insisted on dragging me off to Europe to see the sights: Paris, Venice, Florence, the usual things. Bored the pants off me, till one day, sitting on a lump of rock beside the Parthenon, watching the tourists milling about, clicking their cameras, talking to each other in umpteen languages, it suddenly struck me: tourism is the new world religion. Catholics, Protestants, Hindus, Muslims, Buddhists, atheists – the one thing they have in common is they all believe in the importance of seeing the Parthenon. Or the Sistine Chapel, or the Eiffel Tower. I decided to make it my PhD subject. (David Lodge, *Paradise News*)

What strikes the ambitious, ironic, career-minded academic Roger Sheldrake in David Lodge's satirical novel of 1991, *Paradise News*, had similarly struck the ambitious, career-minded, ironic young journalist, Samuel Clemens, a hundred and thirty-two years earlier, when he subtitled his second and most successful published book "the New Pilgrims' Progress." In 1867, Clemens was commissioned by a San Francisco newspaper, *The Daily Alta California*, to write a series of humorous letters and sketches from abroad. He embarked on "the great pleasure excursion to Europe and the Holy Land"[1] that would provide the materials for *The Innocents Abroad* (1869). Aboard the *Quaker City*, he met and befriended Charles Langdon, who later introduced Clemens to his sister, Olivia, the great love of Clemens's life. Olivia refused Clemens's initial marriage proposal and would not consent until Clemens had secured some measure of what one of Clemens's later fictional protagonists, Huckleberry Finn, termed "respectability." The publication in 1869 of *The Innocents Abroad*, which became an immediate bestseller, provided a substantial measure of financial security, and the two were married the following year. Like Sheldrake, Clemens would build a (sometimes profitable) career out of his combined infatuation and disdain for the tourist hordes which he was a part of. Like Sheldrake's, Clemens's interest in writing about tourism was occasioned in the face of his own anxiety about an impending marriage, the need to make a steady income, and the attendant crisis of becoming "respectable." As with his literary heir, Lodge, satire became Clemens's stock in trade, and provided a way to navigate the perils of his own ambivalence about class, popular literature, and the commodification of experience.

As a popular travelogue and the best-selling travel book of the nineteenth century, *The Innocents Abroad* both signals and documents the emergence of mass culture in post-Civil War American life. Package tourism and its literary analogue, middlebrow popular literature, were twin commodities within the growing industries of commercialized leisure that marketed themselves to new business and professional classes of the prospering and expanding nation. Each participated in shaping a consciousness that was as much collective and national as it was individualist and consumerist. Secular cosmopolitanism, paradoxically enough, breeds national consciousness, as John Carlos Rowe has asserted. Such writings elaborated "the complex relation between U.S. imperialism as it worked to expand national territory and functioned within that territory to consolidate the idea of nation."[2] Americans abroad are confirmed in their Americanness; American travelers in North America exercise their rights and powers over the land. Other critics assent: "American travel writers attempted to define their own country," note Susan Castillo and David Steed, "by commenting [...] on how different it was to the places they visited in their travels."[3] So too does the representation of "tramping" or "roughing it" – Clemens's terms for his romanticized vagabondage – help to establish secure and productive class identities. It was through reading practices and the development of habits of leisure that consumers came to know and identify themselves as American and as stable members of the prosperous middle class.

Mark Twain worked in popular modes, and deliberately cultivated a mass middlebrow audience. Describing his own work in a letter to Andrew Lang, he commented that "I have never tried in even one single instance, to help cultivate the cultivated classes. I was not equipped for it, either by native gifts or training. And I never had any ambition in that direction, but always hunted for bigger game – the masses."[4] Twain's travel writing proved much more popular with his peers than the novels for which he was subsequently remembered. His career as a popular writer is co-extensive with – and codependent on – the inauguration of mass tourism, an industry he both endorses and skewers in *The Innocents Abroad*, which recounts the 1867 voyage of the *Quaker City* to the Mediterranean and the Holy Land and in which the persona of "Mark Twain" emerges, almost fully-formed. *Innocents Abroad* sold over 70,000 copies in its first year, and more than 100,000 in its first three years.[5] Twain was to write four more travel books over the course of his career. He followed *Innocents Abroad* with *Roughing It* (1872), an account of his adventures between 1861 and 1867 in the American Wild West and trips on the Pacific Ocean. *A Tramp Abroad* (1880) described journeys in Germany and central and southern Europe. One of his most endearing books, *Life on the Mississippi* (1883), told of his apprenticeship as a steamboat captain. Towards the end of his life, he produced *Following the Equator: a Trip around the World, or More Tramps Abroad* (1897), a tour of the British Empire. Though he turned to travel writing whenever he was in need of finances, Twain claimed to "loathe to travel, except on foot,"[6] and recounted in a 1900 interview that

> I have made thirty-four long journeys in my life, and thirty-two of them were made under the spur of absolute compulsion. [...] There always was an imperative reason. I had to gather material for books or sketches, I had to stump around lecturing to make money, or I had to go abroad for the health or education of my family. For love of travel – never any of these thirty two journeys. There is no man living who cares less about seeing new places and peoples than I.[7]

He spent over a decade living abroad, and crossed the Atlantic twenty-seven times. Until William Dean Howells was able to certify Twain's work as "literature" – part of Howells's own project of defending a democratic and vernacular realism – Twain's own literary reputation, even celebrity, at the time was based on his travel writing.

And the nineteenth century was the great age of the genre. American readers cultivated a taste for descriptions of American scenes and of life abroad. The critic Benjamin Moran observed in 1859 that "this would seem to be the age of *travel literature*, judging from the many narratives now published, and the general excellence of such work."[8] Richard H. Gassan stresses the centrality of popular travel writing to promoting, for example, tourism in the Hudson Valley and upstate New York: "Tourism became a common literary motif of the mid-1820s, as new authors, in particular, wrote stories featuring tourism in an effort to give their writing a fashionable edge."[9] James Fenimore Cooper worked fashionable destinations into the settings of his 1826 *Last of the Mohicans,* which was consciously designed to shore up his flagging popularity. Washington Irving and others in the Knickerbocker school (Kirke Paulding) made their fortunes as travel writers, as did such popular novelists as Catherine Maria Sedgwick. There was a burgeoning market for tour guides. Travel writing, it seems, allows a distinctly American genius to emerge. Moran continues: "No nation has given more good books of this class to the world since 1820 than the United States, considered with regard to styles or information."[10] Harold Smith estimates that more than 2,000 books about foreign travel alone were published in the U.S. before 1900.[11] Travel writing was a way for writers to make a living, and, alongside literary journals and magazines marked the professionalization of letters in the nineteenth century. As Patricia Jasen points out in her study of literature and the formation of a tourist industry in Ontario, "tourists, unlike most settlers, gloried in the sense of something alien, such as a wilderness that could be enjoyed physically and imaginatively, and then left behind"[12] – like a book. Both forms market experience, reflect upon it, and make it accessible and easily digestible.

Nor was it simply trips abroad that excited readers' interests. If middle-class Americans in the years after the Civil War came to know and performatively identify themselves as American in encounters with Europe, then a market for internal travel (and travel guides and memoirs about the North American continent) had been growing since the eighteen-twenties. As Marguerite Shaffer notes,

> tourism, defined as a kind of virtuous consumption, promised to reconcile this national mythology, which celebrated nature, democracy, and liberty, with the realities of an urban industrial nation-state, dependent on extraction, consumption, and hierarchy […]. […] [T]ourism, as a form of consumption, allowed white, native-born middle- and upperclass Americans to escape the social and cultural confines of everyday life to a liminal space where they could temporarily reimagine themselves as heroic or authentic figures.[13]

Gassan documents the ways in which the American tourist industry that emerged between 1810 and 1820 centered around the Hudson River Valley and, particularly after 1821, Saratoga Springs, the Niagara region, and

Upper Canada. By 1833, promoters of the industry boast that "technology had transformed the journey into something that almost everybody could afford."[14] After the eighteen-seventies, the history of American tourism reflects a "shift from eastern resort vacations and the European Grand Tour toward transcontinental travel,"[15] primarily to the west, about which Twain also wrote extensively.

My claim, in short, is that mass literature and mass tourism developed mutually and interdependently, concomitant with the emergence of culture industries marketing themselves to the newly leisured middle classes. Assessing Twain's travel writing with an eye to its tacit, if satiric, solicitation of middlebrow audiences I want briefly to highlight the mutual interdependence of mass literature and mass tourism within the broader spectrum of a newly minted American popular culture.

By the eighteen-fifties, historian David Daniel Kilbride points out, "[g]oing overseas became easier, cheaper, and more comfortable as it became like any other commodity."[16] Throughout *Innocents Abroad*, Twain stresses that the tour is "a pleasure trip," more a "picnic" than an adventure, and comments on how very "well advertised" (18) was the expedition. He satirizes, too, the over-reaching class aspirations of his fellow voyagers, who will seemingly be excited to rub elbows with 'royalty' in Europe. Twain targets as well the paltry efforts made by the shipping line to confer a spurious status on their customers: "the company to be rigidly selected by a pitiless 'Committee on Applications'" he notes, excitedly, as he hurries to make his application; after purchasing his ticket, he is delighted by "the novelty of being 'select'" (22).

Twain notes too, that, sadly, neither Henry Ward Beecher nor General Sherman were able to make the trip, though they had wished to; "a popular actress had entered her name on the ship's books, but something interfered and *she* [emphasis in the text] couldn't go" (23). Twain's readers, like his fellow travelers, are in on the joke. Package tourism, it turns out, is a peculiarly disingenuous and potentially ironic form of conspicuous consumption. Twain winkingly mocks and derides the tourists' pretensions to 'class.'

As with popular literature, mass tourism was, from the very beginnings of the package tour, disparaged for its populist appeal. Critics targeted the presumed boorishness of middle-class travelers, the commodification of sublime experience to those unprepared for it, and highlighted the presumed inauthenticity of 'tourism.' Citing an 1848 editorial in *Blackwood's Magazine* disparaging the ways in which mass travel "spoils all rational travel," Jeffrey Alan Melton documents the suspicion of "mass tourism": "it repels the student, the philosopher, and the manly investigator, from subjects which have been thus trampled into mire by the hoofs of a whole tribe of traveling bipeds."[17]

As an ambivalent promoter of both popular literature and middle-class tourism, Twain's ironic narratives negotiate these tensions perfectly. On the one hand, they indulge and gently lampoon the figure of the 'ugly American,' while at the same time bathetically skewering the pretensions of 'culture' and satirizing the sacramental allure of the exotic. In his study of Twain's travel writing, Harold Hellwig, who describes *Innocents* as a "parody" of popular guidebooks, demonstrates how "'the personal narrative' [...] creates the identity of the travelling author, an invented guise, the identity of a journalist who reports truthfully what he encounters in his travels and then undercuts the notion that this journalist can be trusted;"[18] thus travel writing is key to the development of Twain's ironic mode, and the manufacture of his labile persona.

Twain's humorous method proceeds along two tracks. His conceit is to take conventional generic formulae and to repeat them to the point where they are exposed as clichés, made ridiculous. Second, Twain generates humor by juxtaposing the romantic with the banal; in travel writing, this means pairing exaggerated expectations of the sublime with bathetic descriptions of the underwhelming experience.

At one point, for example, as the pilgrims enter the Holy Land, Twain describes "the little execrable village of Baniyas" (337) where Christ gave to Peter the keys to the Kingdom of Heaven. He is overcome with the expected feeling of sublimity:

> I cannot comprehend yet that I am sitting where a god has stood, and looking upon the brook and the mountains which that god looked upon, and am surrounded by dusky men and women whose ancestors saw him, and even talked with him, face to face, and carelessly, just as they would have done with any other stranger. I cannot comprehend this; the gods of my understanding have been always hidden in clouds and very far away. (339)

Immediately, however, the next paragraph juxtaposes this realization – one of the rarer moments in the text where he seems not to have his tongue in his cheek – with Twain's rather offensive comments on the squalor of the native Arab population: "that morning, during breakfast, the usual assemblage of squalid humanity sat patiently without the charmed circle of the camp and waited for such crumbs as pity might bestow upon their misery" (339).

The passage grows more and more complicated and circuitous. Twain's sympathies begin to waver as he contends with the immense difficulty of confronting this alien and purportedly primitive people and effectively describing them for his readers. He is reminded, at first, of their similarity to American Indians:

> They reminded me of Indians, did these people. They had but little clothing, but such as they had was fanciful in character and fantastic in its arrangement. Any little absurd gewgaw or gimcrack they had disposed in such a way as to make it attract attention most readily. They sat in silence, and with tireless patience watched our every motion with that vile, uncomplaining impoliteness which is so truly Indian, and which makes a white man so nervous and uncomfortable and savage that he wants to exterminate the whole tribe. (340)

Note the inversion in the last sentence and the complex layering and shifting of ironical perspective. Although Twain confesses to sharing the same nervousness felt by other whites when confronted with implacable racial difference, he also subtly indicts his own exaggerated genocidal response. Anglo-Americans are rendered "savage" in this encounter; Indians are merely impolite. Recall that this is penned in 1868, at the time when the debates about the 'pacification' of the Plains tribes were heating up. In the next paragraphs, Twain is moved to pity, rather than barbarism, and takes the occasion to satirize a sentimentalized understanding of Indians by presenting the harsh realities of their living conditions:

> These people about us had other peculiarities which I have noticed in the noble red man, too: they were infested with vermin, and the dirt had caked on them till it amounted to bark.
>
> The little children were in a pitiable condition – they all had sore eyes, and were otherwise afflicted in various ways. (340)

In the end, as is so often the case in Twain's writing, a Yankee pragmatism, tempered with a small dose of Christian charity, helps to ease (without fully resolving) the impasse. A member of the party, Dr. B., "in the charity of his nature" (340), treats a young child. As word spread that there is medicine to be had, the Arabs swarm the doctor for further treatment: "When each individual got his portion of medicine, his eyes were radiant with joy – notwithstanding by nature they are a thankless and impassive race" (341). Twain recalls too that "Christ knew how to preach to these simple, superstitious, disease tortured creatures" (341), and that, for his labors and ministrations, Christ too was taken advantage of. Twain ends the chapter by comically describing the shabby condition of his horse, and decides that Arabs should not be sentimentalized, for they are cruel to their animals.

Such techniques served Twain well – the comic contrast between the romantic and the everyday (or the exotic and the 'American') drives such classic Twain narratives as *The Adventures of Tom Sawyer* (1876) or *A Connecticut Yankee in King Arthur's Court* (1889), and, indeed, is key to the generation of literary realism. Twain is sometimes classed among the realists, though he is an odd bird in the company of such turn-of-the-century masters of the form as Henry James, William Dean Howells, Edith Wharton, or Willa Cather. But his work typifies the genealogy of realism, a form of writing that cannot come to exist or to know itself as 'realist' except with romance as its foil. Twain's method involves setting up a romantic point of view, then undercutting it. And just as the reader expects the sober, objective appraisal to supplant the perspective lampooned, Twain undercuts sobriety and realism, demonstrating how self-interested such a stance can also be.

A too easily purchased realism, it turns out, is for Twain as inadequate a response to the complexities of the human situation as is a ready romanticism. What we are left with in a typical passage of Twain's prose is an endless diminuendo of irony that defers ever taking a definitive point of view towards its subject matter. A stance is taken, and undercut; a new stance emerges and in turn is undermined; this continues, and could in theory continue without end, until some occasion – or, if not, an opportunity for Twain to end a scene with such remarks as "at any rate" or "as I was saying" – provides a convenient excuse for the narrator to make a laughing withdrawal from a scene of cultural antagonism that cannot be resolved.

What grows out of this, ultimately, is less a point of view than a persona – Mark Twain – complicit, but knowing, savage, but benignly humorous, mercurial and amused, largely uncommitted, but not untouched by passion, who combines levity with rapaciousness. An American, in short, even an ideal American.

Twain can be read, notes Ann Ryan, as "the original voice of America, exposing the sham of Europe's cultural hegemony and the detritus of its history."[19] In *Innocents*, American travelers come to know and identify themselves *as American* in these confrontations with Europe and the Holy land. Examples from the text are numerous. Here is a rich exchange between one of Twain's companions and a guide in Genoa, who has targeted their group as seemingly easy prey:

> Ah, what did you say this gentlemen's name was?
>
> Christopher Colombo. Ze great Christopher Colombo!
>
> Christopher Colombo. The great Christopher Colombo. Well, what did *he* do?
>
> Discover America! Discover America, oh, ze devil!
>
> Discover America. No – that statement will hardly wash. We are just from America ourselves. We heard nothing about it. Christopher Colombo – pleasant name – is he dead?
>
> Oh, corpo di Baccho! Three hundred year!
>
> What did he die of?
>
> I do not know! I cannot tell.
>
> Smallpox, think?
>
> I do not know, genteelmen! I do not know *what* he die of!
>
> Measles, likely?
>
> Maybe – maybe – I do *not* know – I think he die of somethings.
>
> Parents living?
>
> Im-posseeble!
>
> Ah – which is the bust and which is the pedestal?
>
> Santa Maria! *Zis* ze bust! *Zis* ze pedestal!
>
> Ah, I see, I see – happy combination – very happy combination indeed. Is – is this the first time this gentleman was ever on a bust?
>
> The joke was lost on the foreigner – guides cannot master the subtleties of an American joke. (211; emphasis in the text)

Travel writing was part of a larger project constructing and securing American identity. As Twain observes later, his aim in *Innocents* was to turn the tables on European visitors to the US:

> Immediately after the War of 1812, tourists began to come to America, from England; scattering ones at first, then a sort of procession of them – a procession which kept up its plodding, patient march through the land

during many, many years. Each tourist took notes, and went home and published a book – a book which was usually calm, truthful, reasonable, kind; but which seemed just the reverse to our tender-footed progenitors.[20]

And he lampooned, as he liked to do, their writings: "it is a pretty crude literature for a man accustomed to handling a pen."[21] Twain wanted to do better, to write better – more scathingly – of Europe than Europeans wrote of America. As Charles Neider observes, he had little taste for adventure or exoticism, and was more comfortable as a tourist: "he was on the whole a conventional traveler who treasured his comforts and was content to go where others had gone before."[22] Much of the joke of *A Tramp Abroad*, for example, is that Twain's announced arduous expedition through Europe on foot takes place largely by rail; such comfortable accommodations reflect the accessibility of leisure. In a comic twist, the only real 'tramps' Twain encounters turn out to be aristocrats, as he discovers when he later encounters them at the opera.

The invention of the American, the construction of a leisure class, the fabrication of the persona of Mark Twain as a charismatic 'voice of America,' and the expansion of the market for a calculated popular literature – all four projects are inextricably aligned and entwined. It is not my purpose here to examine Twain's Yankee vernacular – also central to his cultivation of middle-class Americana. Nor do I aim to analyze his growing disenchantment with the American experiment in his later years. We should propose that the later hardening of Twain's innate skepticism into a mature critical consciousness was an outgrowth of his development as a travel writer. Ann Ryan, who sees Twain as a fundamentally urban author (though he wrote little about city life per se), notes how his homespun performance is key to the parochial global poles of his persona, and tied to an emerging American modernism, urbanism, and imperialism, even as his own critical politics became increasingly "cosmopolitan": "sympathetic, engaged, yet also distant." [23] These developments involve the "transformation," as Alan Gribben and Jeffrey Alan Melton note, of both tourism – from something only people of substantial wealth could afford into popular packages available to an increasingly middle-class market for leisure – and writing, where Twain is able to manufacture the "quintessentially 'American' qualities"[24] for which he was to become known.

Notes

[1] Mark Twain (1966 [1869]). *The Innocents Abroad, or the New Pilgrims' Progress*. New York: Harper, 17. Further references to this edition will be included in the text.
[2] John Carlos Rowe (2000). *Literary Culture and U.S. Imperialism: From the Revolution to World War II.* New York: Oxford University Press, 5.
[3] Susan Castillo and David Steed (2009). "Introduction." *American Travel and Empire*. Liverpool: Liverpool University Press, 3 (1-8).
[4] Mark Twain, qtd. in: Jeffrey Alan Melton (2002). *Mark Twain, Travel Books, and Tourism: The Tale of a Great Popular Movement.* Tuscaloosa: University of Alabama Press, 2.
[5] Melton (2002), 1.
[6] Mark Twain, qtd. in: Charles Neider (2000 [1961]). "Introduction." *The Travels of Mark Twain*. Ed. C. N. New York: Cooper Square, 9 (9-24).
[7] Mark Twain, qtd. in: *Ibid.*, 23.
[8] Benjamin Moran, qtd. in: Alan Gribben and Jeffrey Alan Melton (2009). "Introduction." *Mark Twain on the Move*. Eds. A. G. and J. A. M. Tuscaloosa: University of Alabama Press, xi (xi-xx).
[9] Richard H. Gassan (2008). *The Birth of American Tourism: New York, The Hudson Valley, and American Culture, 1790-1830.* Amherst: University of Massachusetts Press, 109.
[10] Benjamin Moran, qtd. in Gribben and Melton (2009), xi.
[11] Harold Smith, qtd. in: *Ibid.*
[12] Patricia Jasen (1995). *Wild Things; Nature, Culture, and Tourism in Ontario, 1790-1914.* Toronto: University of Toronto Press, 25.
[13] Marguerite S. Shaffer (2001). *See America First: Tourism and National Identity, 1880-1940*. Washington, D.C.: Smithsonian, 5.
[14] Gassan (2008), 21.
[15] *Ibid.*
[16] Daniel Kilbride (2013). *Being American in Europe, 1750-1860*. Baltimore, MD: Johns Hopkins University Press, 5.
[17] Melton (2002), 6.
[18] Harold H. Hellwig (2008). *Mark Twain's Travel Literature: The Odyssey of a Mind.* Jefferson, NC: McFarland, 15.
[19] Ann M. Ryan (2008). "Mark Twain and the Cosmopolitan Ideal." *Cosmopolitan Twain*. Eds. A. M. R. and Joseph B. McCullough. Columbia: University of Missouri Press, 2 (1-20).
[20] Mark Twain (1967). *Life on the Mississippi. The Complete Travel Books of Mark Twain. Volume 2: The Later Works.* Ed. Charles Neider. Garden City: Doubleday, 488 (347-665).

[21] *Ibid.*, 490.
[22] Charles Neider (2000 [1961]), 24.
[23] Ryan (2008), 10.
[24] Gribben/Melton (2009), xiv.

Bibliography

Castillo, Susan, and David Seed (2009). "Introduction." *American Travel and Empire*. Liverpool: Liverpool University Press, 1-8.

Gassan, Richard H. (2008). *The Birth of American Tourism: New York, The Hudson Valley, and American Culture, 1790-1830.* Amherst: University of Massachusetts Press.

Gribben, Alan, and Jeffrey Alan Melton (2009). "Introduction." *Mark Twain on the Move*. Eds. A. G. and J. A. M. Tuscaloosa: University of Alabama Press, xi-xx.

Hellwig, Harold H. (2008). *Mark Twain's Travel Literature: The Odyssey of a Mind.* Jefferson, NC: McFarland.

Jasen, Patricia (1995). *Wild Things; Nature, Culture, and Tourism in Ontario, 1790-1914.* Toronto: University of Toronto Press.

Kilbride, Daniel (2013). *Being American in Europe, 1750-1860*. Baltimore, MD: Johns Hopkins University Press.

Melton, Jeffrey Alan (2002). *Mark Twain, Travel Books, and Tourism: The Tale of a Great Popular Movement.* Tuscaloosa: University of Alabama Press.

Neider, Charles (2000 [1961]). "Introduction." *The Travels of Mark Twain*. Ed. C. N. New York: Cooper Square, 9-24.

Rowe, John Carlos (2000). *Literary Culture and U.S. Imperialism: From the Revolution to World War II.* New York: Oxford University Press.

Ryan, Ann M., and Joseph B. McCullough (eds.) (2008). *Cosmopolitan Twain*. Columbia: University of Missouri Press.

Ryan, Ann M. (2008). "Mark Twain and the Cosmopolitan Ideal." *Cosmopolitan Twain*. Eds. A. M. R. and Joseph B. McCullough. Columbia: University of Missouri Press, 1-20.

Shaffer, Marguerite S. (2001). *See America First: Tourism and National Identity, 1880-1940*. Washington, D.C.: Smithsonian.

Twain, Mark (2009). *Mark Twain on the Move: A Travel Reader*. Eds. Alan Gribben and Jeffrey Alan Melton. Tuscaloosa: University of Alabama Press.

--- (2000 [1961]). *The Travels of Mark Twain*. Ed. Charles Neider. New York: Cooper Square.

--- (1967). *Following the Equator. The Complete Travel Books of Mark Twain. Vol. 2.* Ed. Charles Neider. Garden City: Doubleday, 667-1084.

--- (1967). *Life on the Mississippi. The Complete Travel Books of Mark Twain. Volume 2: The Later Works*. Ed. Charles Neider. Garden City: Doubleday, 347-665.

--- (1966 [1869]). *The Innocents Abroad, or the New Pilgrims' Progress*. New York: Harper.

William M. Decker (Oklahoma State University)

Consuming Europe: *Daisy Miller* and the Package Tour

Spurred by a hubristic confidence in the dollar, Americans en masse after the Civil War extended their consumption well beyond the national border.[1] They did so commonly with a sense of entitlement, one that expected the world to speak English and generally conform to American tastes. Then as now, they preferred experience that came in packages with contents clearly listed. Granted, no trip is complete without its random element – the list should include an "off-road" option and "dark stranger" possibility – but package-tour shoppers crave guarantees that travelers will return intact and essentially unchanged. The promotional circular for the Quaker City Cruise that Mark Twain reproduces almost verbatim in the first chapter of *The Innocents Abroad* abundantly measures the package preference. Assuring voyagers that "[a]n experienced physician will be on board," the advertisement teases with prospects of viewing the Mediterranean belt of fire:

> Skirting along the north coast of Sicily, passing through the group of Aeolian Isles, in sight of Stromboli and Vulcania, both active volcanoes, through the Straits of Messina, with 'Scylla' on the one hand and 'Charybdis' on the other, along the east coast of Sicily, and in sight of Mount Etna,[2]

passengers may find themselves in proximity to sites of catastrophic spectacle but at a secure and regulated distance. They can buy into an experience of simulated danger, and if the product is as good as advertised they may momentarily lose sight of the simulation. But actual risk is low. Industrial tourism, then as now, appeals to the risk averse.

Mark Twain and Henry James are similarly critical of the mass-market fetish of safe programmed travel and the American tourist's appalling tendency to haul village comforts and accustomed routines along when abroad. Both wince at their fellow citizens' display of presumption and ignorance. Both are skeptical of the package tours that seduce down-home Americans across the sea. Yet as authors and businessmen, both profit from the tourism they decry and both are deeply complicit in the packaging process. Both encourage tourism on a mass scale notwithstanding their generally satiric treatment of the American consumer abroad. Both understand that the traveling public overlaps with the reading public and that readers are eager to laugh at themselves but only when presented with an image of qualified likeness. Both thus concede the power of the dollar to shape the satire of dollar consumerism. Focusing on *Daisy Miller* this essay will examine this curious symbiosis and the ways in which James accordingly creates in Daisy an iconic and ultimately admirative image of the adolescent female consumer, always shopping, always on tour.

First, however, I would like to linger over the term "package tour." Pleasure excursions have long been conceived as package propositions. The British "Grand Tour," from the sixteenth century forward, comprised an assortment of destinations and activities, more or less scripted and predictable of result, supposed to finish the young gentleman's classical education while affording vent to his riotous energies.[3] Before the Grand Tour the Christian pilgrimage – to Canterbury, Lourdes, or all the way to Jerusalem – combined sacred purpose with secular distraction. But the term "package tour" really pertains to an era of consumer tourism: the democratization of travel that follows, by a generation or two, the industrial revolution's massive production and distribution of wealth, an affluence that provides an increasing number of people with leisure time and the means to fill it. "Package tour" pertains to a travel industry that evolves relative to such leisure and that does so through class-coded marketing. In short, it underscores the retailing of the travel experience as a particular mark of leisure and prestige. Published in 1878, *Daisy Miller* constitutes a subtle index not only of the fate of an American family ill-prepared for the perils of Europe but also of a travel industry that, drawing on Lord Byron, Edward Gibbon, and C. F. Volney (among others), bundles an itinerary that puts the comparatively illiterate Daisy on the road to a moonlit but malarial Coliseum. James, I believe, understands perfectly the literary dimensions of an industry whose retail activities depend absolutely on the telling and re-telling of travelers' tales. This industry counts among its eager participants the consumer of travel literature. Travel and travel literature predate modern tourism, but the travel industry had formed by the time James published his first travel sketches and transatlantic tales. To Thomas Cooke, to Murray, Baedeker, Harper and Appleton, the literary practice of a Henry James exists in ancillary relation. Package tour and literary ware depend on a common economy.

From an American perspective the European tour always existed as a distinct if variable experience ripe for mass marketing. In modest numbers Americans had crossed the Atlantic for business and pleasure from the colonial period forward. Through much of the nineteenth century, privileged young men, imitating the English aristocratic pattern, embarked on a post-baccalaureate European trawl (London to Paris, Paris to Rome, with an occasional sojourn in transcendental Germany) before settling into the sedentary rounds of professional and family life. Variants of the tour might serve as physical and psychological therapy (one thinks of Emerson, for instance, sailing to Europe soon after his first wife's death). Men and women of artistic and literary calling established residencies in European capitals. So did small colonies of leisured Americans who could afford to live where and how they chose or who, finding themselves in reduced financial circumstances, might live well and cheaply in the European countryside. James Fenimore Cooper, Washington Irving, Nathaniel Hawthorne, and Margaret Fuller all spent productive years living abroad as did nearly every significant painter and sculptor of the early national period. Henry James's father, Henry James, Sr., inherited from his father a moderate fortune that allowed him to pursue a life of philosophical inquiry and to indulge his own nomadic inclinations. The novelist's childhood European experiences took place at a time when the American in Europe belonged to an elite – an intellectual and artistic if not always a moneyed elite.

Following the Civil War, Americans of old money and artistic aspiration were joined by upwardly mobile fellow citizens whose European excursions were facilitated by the general rise and distribution of wealth, steady advances in steamship technology, and a travel industry that had developed affordable package tours. During the first half of the century, two thousand to eight thousand Americans annually crossed the Atlantic to Europe; after the Civil War, the figure soared to forty thousand.[4] In *The Innocents Abroad,* after ridiculing the circular promoting the *Quaker City* tour, Twain sheepishly observes that "[e]verybody was going to Europe – I, too, was going to Europe. Everybody was going to the famous Paris

Exposition – I, too, was going to the Paris Exposition."[5] For his part, having traveled to and resided in Europe in advance of the crowd, Henry James noted disparagingly the arrival of newcomers. Embarked, in 1869, on a first solo tour, James felt mortified by the hordes of Americans for whom European travel served chiefly to confirm the superiority of everything American. Writing to his mother, he appears distinctly unsympathetic with the lot of his culturally narrow countrymen and women:

> Their ignorance – their stingy, defiant, grudging attitude towards everything European – their perpetual reference of all things to some American standard or precedent which exists only in their own unscrupulous windbags – and then our unhappy poverty of voice, of speech, and of physiognomy – these things glare at you hideously.[6]

Yet like Twain he would soon perceive the humor as well as the profitability of this tourist phenomenon and in Daisy exhibit a softening and sympathetic conception of the popular trend.

Daisy Miller is a twice-told, a retold, tale. It derives from gossip about an American girl in Rome that James's friend Alice Bartlett reported to him in 1872.[7] As gossip narrative, the story concerned a young American woman, naïve and nouveau-riche, smitten by the attention of Italian fortune-hunting men. As in the novella, the girl's flirtatious behavior scandalizes and embarrasses the old-money expatriate community. We do not know whether, as James heard it from Alice Bartlett, the story also concerned a clueless mother or a homesick younger brother, but if a fatal late-night visit to the Coliseum had been part of the storyline, we almost certainly would have some record of that. Eight years later, when James wrote the tale, there were other sources that he freely drew upon. Winterbourne, for example, displaced to Geneva as a child, and long naturalized to an expatriate existence, builds upon the Henry James life narrative. Aunt Costello and Mrs. Walker, as arbiters of American conduct abroad, might reflect any number of rich anti-republican expatriate Americans James may have known in his youth. As for Daisy's mother and brother, they could resemble scores of Americans James observed, exemplifying as they do an "ignorance," a "stingy, defiant, grudging attitude towards everything European," as well as an "unhappy poverty of voice, of speech, and of physiognomy."[8] Mrs. Miller epitomizes the package tourist in her insistence that activities conform to a script, whether it be Harper's, Appleton's, and Murray's guide to Europe or some other American tourist's advice on what and what not to see. While in Vevey, for example, she takes no interest in the Château de Chillon as it does not appear on the Castle Master List. As she says, speaking like a true consumer, "we only want to see the principal ones."[9] Later, after the action has shifted to Rome, Winterbourne asks Mrs. Miller "how she was pleased with Rome." Mrs. Miller is candid: "I must say I am disappointed… We had heard so much about it; I suppose we had heard too much. But we couldn't help that. We had been led to expect something different" (62). (The passage reads like a page from *The Innocents Abroad*; all that remains is for Mrs. Miller to complain of being "swindled.") That "something different" is never specified, but it might have been something other than the transitional rough-edged Rome of the late eighteen-seventies, the energized center of a newly unified Italy and no longer the seat of the Papal States, now reduced to the circumscribed enclave of Vatican City. Mrs. Miller, we may presume, favors a clean street. The sanitary infrastructure of eighteen-seventies Rome could not have met her standards.

Daisy of course is likewise a package tourist, albeit one who in the list of tour contents looks for Romance if not Danger. She is naturally impatient of the guided tour. To her, the Château de Chillon is simply "that old castle" (44), a pasteboard image without history or poetry (she knows nothing of Byron's commemoration of that history in "The Prisoner of Chillon"). Physically and socially robust in contrast with her lethargic mother, however, she is eager to visit the Château in the company of the doting Winterbourne, losing interest in the trip only when she senses that Winterbourne has a European girlfriend whom he finds more compelling than herself. But her tourist enthusiasms re-kindle when she arrives in the eternal city. Neither a student of the past nor of history-in-the-making, Daisy is nonetheless heartily pleased with Rome. "It's a great deal nicer than I thought," she tells Winterbourne.

> I thought it would be fearfully quiet; I was sure it would be awfully poky. I was sure we should be going round all the time with one of those dreadful old men that explain about the pictures and things. But we only had about a week of that, and now I'm enjoying myself. (66)

Impatient of one kind of package, she has availed herself of another and explains that her enjoyment derives from "the society," international and "extremely select" (66). It is evident to Winterbourne that, as his aunt had reported, this girl with the pretty American teeth has become the magnet for a bevy of Italian fortune hunters. As package tourist she is an easy mark, and as such her adventures may appear to reprise a tale that preexists her arrival. Yet it is here that James's intervention – his retelling of an old tale – constitutes a signal event, as he chooses to exempt Daisy from reduction to a known storyline, one that would confirm her ignorance and bad taste as well as her adolescent female silliness. He exempts her from the scorn heaped on the figure of her mother and the hordes of arriving package tourists. He exempts her, moreover, at the expense of Mrs. Costello and Mrs. Walker, as well as of Frederick Winterbourne, who are made to look uncharitable, obtuse, and culturally obsolete. In lifting Daisy above their suspicions and strictures he roundly admonishes the tourist reader whom he has nonetheless tempted to judge Daisy harshly. In short he chooses to develop a character that does not reduce to a figure in a titillating cautionary tale and in doing so creates a fresh literary personality, a new narrative product. The novelty of Daisy lends itself to her supreme marketability as the type of a new tourist heroine.[10]

Since the days of Charlotte and Lucy Temple, Anglo-American girls had been seduced and American heiresses pursued by the sons of a ruined European aristocracy. Daisy comes from a long line of fallen – or shall we say falling? – women. But it is important to note that for *Daisy Miller*'s author and first readers, whose social affiliations correspond far more with Winterbourne, Mrs. Costello, and Mrs. Walker than with the Millers, Daisy's naïve and self-assertive behavior constitutes an innovative pattern. In 1878 Daisy is a new kind of person and her novelty is both demographic and literary. Demographically, she represents a young American female whose father's recently acquired wealth provides her with leisured alternatives to early marriage, farm work, or life as a mill hand or domestic.[11] Like generations of middle-class American teenagers who have come of age since the end of World War II, but unlike all but a few young people in post-Civil War America, Daisy has opportunities to socialize, shop, and venture beyond the authority of her not-very-authoritarian parents. Well might this figure strike us as a prophecy of affluent and prolonged adolescence, core engine of a consumer economy. Literarily, she is absolutely fresh: the creature of the "realist" tendency in post-Civil War fiction dedicated to examining a democratizing and rapidly evolving social order, one that generates novel forms of personhood that defy comprehension by the old class codes. The most prominent early representation of the blonde mainstream "American girl," Daisy serves as prototype of the beach movie ingénue and boy-crazy teen. The fact that we meet her on vacation is significant. As James had depicted Christopher Newman the year before in *The American*, and as he would portray Isabel Archer, heroine of *The Portrait of a Lady*, three years later, he presents Daisy not as she might be found at home in the small industrial hinterland city, but as one who has already crossed an ocean and a national border or two – as someone wholly given to the era's unprecedented social and geographic circulation.

The reader of 1878, if unprepared to recognize this girl, knows something of that circulation – the volitional mobility of the affluent. The opening sentences indicate that James envisions his audience either as a leisured and touring lot or as people who aspire to leisure and travel. "At the little town of Vevey, in Switzerland, there is a particularly comfortable hotel," he begins, sketching a contemporary industrial vacation scene. "There are," he continues, "indeed, many hotels, for the entertainment of tourists is the business of the place, which, as many travelers will remember, is seated upon the edge of a remarkably blue lake – a lake that it behooves every tourist to visit" (35). Not every reader will have had occasion to remember this lake, but James can assume that his audience possesses a familiarity with travel and resort stays, and they will want to read mildly scandalous stories situated in such settings. He proceeds to describe the range of hotels that line the shore from "'the grand hotel' of the newest fashion" to "the little Swiss pension of an elder day" catering to an international clientele among whom, "in the month of June, American travelers are extremely numerous" (35-36). The language of this paragraph seems lifted from a tour guide. It evokes the rapid development of a formerly exclusive summer retreat into a broadly commercial recreation site, patronized by newly moneyed classes who are buying their way into erstwhile aristocratic preserves. Readers in 1878 were thus prompted to locate themselves somewhere along this privileged spectrum. After providing a wide-angle glimpse of Lake Geneva Resort Row, the narrator returns to the "particularly comfortable hotel" mentioned in the first sentence, namely the "Trois Couronnes," an establishment "distinguished from many of its upstart neighbors by an air both of luxury and of maturity" (35). Such qualities, the narrator suggests, may remind American travelers of Ocean House (Newport) and Congress Hall (Saratoga), old-style aristocratic hotels providing hospitality to the young democracy's elite. As socially aspirational period readers, we may think that only the elite should stay at such a place. But in one of the story's initial reversals of expectation, the "Trois Couronnes," the most exclusive hotel in Vevey, patronized by Mrs. Costello, turns out to be the lodging of the upstart Millers who might be thought to prefer a hotel at their level of luxury and maturity: "with a chalk-white front, a hundred balconies, and a dozen flags flying from its roof" (35). Nouveau riche as readers with this sort of experience themselves may be, James makes it easy for them to regard the Millers as rank gate crashers. Daisy and family truly fit the class-inflected definition of that term, but their dollars are as good as anyone's when it comes to consuming European amenities.

Entering what James lays out as the familiarly exotic world of *Daisy Miller*, readers are thus coaxed to self-identify as more or less seasoned travelers of an elite class standing. Where one stays makes a difference, but so too what one does and with what foreknowledge one embraces the travel occasion. Beyond the superficial significance of lodging, *Daisy Miller* unfolds amid a geography deeply shaded by the romantic and generally tragic bearing of European history. The gross ignorance of the Millers begs the question of what individual readers can demonstrate by way of a superior knowledge. They may know hotels and have a rudimentary grasp of castles, but beyond the safety of the illuminated tourist path James sets readers adrift in a perilous and unpackaged terrain – perilous, certainly, beyond the reckoning of either Daisy or Winterbourne. Despite its colonization by arriving hordes and full-service hotels, Europe is not yet homogenized in the manner of a Newport or Saratoga Springs. For James, if not for his reader, each particular European locale evokes historical narratives against which the story of Americans on package tour will always seem lightweight notwithstanding its tragic culmination. But James, I believe, wishes to please as much as to provoke and is willing to collude in what he looks upon as his readership's aversion to tragedy. What happens to Daisy is sad and (from a contemporary perspective) unjust, but having read to the end one continues to laugh at her barbed put-downs of Winterbourne and Mrs. Walker. James nuances the tragic plot in the interest of keeping Daisy Miller (to cite an exemplarily American marketing adjective) "lite." As a participant in a popular literary genre, James's novella proposes that the tragedies of high- and low-born Americans are destined alike to remain of a pathetic cast, almost indeed indistinguishable from their comedies. From Washington Irving to Bill Bryson, American misadventures in Europe tend toward the narrative frame of *National Lampoon's European Vacation*, in whose genealogy I would argue *Daisy Miller* figures centrally. In representing the perilous unpackaged dimensions of Europe, James might have steered straight to the heart of Old World darkness. Instead, he provides a comic cognitive package – one that under its narrative shrinkwrap serves a popular if upwardly-mobile readership.

Daisy captures the Holy Grail of tourist experience, to see the Coliseum by moonlight. Having spent little time familiarizing herself with Roman history and culture ("pictures and things" [66]), it might be argued that her evening in the Coliseum reduces to fulfilling a package checklist. (She has not read *Manfred*, as Winterbourne has, but she still feels something of the poetry as it has come down to her through tour-guide drivel and traveler's tales.) As well, it might be argued that the Millers' European itinerary, their lodging in the most expensive hotels, and their appearance in extravagant clothes – "no," remarks Mrs. Costello to her nephew, marveling over Daisy's fine taste in clothes, "you don't know how well she dresses" (47) – is a textbook example of what Thorstein Veblen termed "conspicuous consumption," more specifically the "vicarious consumption" of a rich man's wife and children (77). But it might also be argued that Daisy brings to the Eternal City a capacity to respond to the allure of the place that reflects James's own youthful susceptibility as well as that of other American youth. In the Rome of this era, to quote Henry Adams, twenty-two at the time of his 1860 visit,

> the lights and shadows were still medieval, and medieval Rome was alive; the shadows breathed and glowed, full of soft forms felt by lost senses. No sand-blast of science had yet skinned off the epidermis of history, thought, and feeling.[12]

Rome was not by any measure "safe." In Adams's description it was "a gospel of anarchy and vice; the last place under the sun for educating the young; yet it was, by common consent, the only spot that the young – of either sex and every race – passionately, perversely, wickedly loved."[13] Writing thus in 1907, Adams provides a key to understanding what might be termed the passion of Daisy Miller. Given the vitality of such youthful response, can old-wealth Americans be said to have any higher motive for sojourning in Rome? In an 1873 letter to his mother written during his second Roman visit, James characterizes the expatriate colony as "without relations with the place, or much serious appreciation of it."[14] Such a comment would seem to apply exactly to the condition of Mrs. Costello and Mrs. Walker and at least in part to Winterbourne. If that is the case, why, except to spend money, are they there? What order of imaginary rank are they looking to buy?

It is a question to consider among the larger contexts of American social and geographical mobility in the nineteenth century. The narrative of westward migration – Europe to America, East Coast to the continental interiors – is associated with liberation from the European past and reinvention of the possibilities of life at both an individual and civic level. But what about the narrative of "return" to Europe? Does it imply a rejection of distinctly American manners, attitudes, and popular culture, all of which Daisy embodies? Does it involve nostalgia for the very social hierarchies Americans have traditionally prided themselves in rejecting? Can Winterbourne, Mrs. Costello, Mrs. Walker, and the Millers explain why they have crossed the Atlantic? For the self-made Christopher Newman of *The American*, the European excursion implements an explicit agenda – to purchase a life of luxury and distinction that formerly one possessed only as a birthright. Where Newman fails, Daniel Touchett of *The Portrait of a Lady* succeeds, having exercised his Yankee banker's acumen to become master of a Thames country house. But except for Daisy, none of the Americans in *Daisy Miller* seems comparably purpose driven – and to be driven by a purpose, however naïve, lends attraction and marketability to the representative American character. If the old-wealth Americans reject the power of popular culture, do the Millers, with Daisy leading the charge, represent an evangelical movement to connect with the soul and soil of Europe and to liberate bourgeois Europeans from their reserved and pokey ways? Can any of these Americans anticipate how, in the course of this experience, they will change, or what transformations they have undergone as a result of an extended residence? Can they go home again, purchases in hand, and, if so, duty free?

The scene in the Protestant Cemetery would appear to answer that question as it pertains to Daisy. The girl has been too bold, has challenged too many conventions, and Europe, to the satisfaction of the old-money Yanks, has had its revenge, consuming Daisy in the process. But as character and commodity Daisy is really too good to kill, or so her resourceful and mercenary creator must have believed. In 1883, James adapted what had been to date his most popular tale for the stage, and in the process decided that Daisy need not die after all. Not only does Daisy not die, but she also successfully detaches Winterbourne from his corrupt European liaisons and general expatriate aimlessness and, taking him by the hand, leads him back to the U.S. where, presumably, they marry and live happily ever after, old wealth reinvigorated by new, united in the conviction that life at home is the more sustainable option. True, the play never found a theater company to produce it, but the very fact that James could thus resurrect, repackage, and repurpose Daisy affirms the fundamentally comic vision of her character as well as the power of her dollar, after all, to deliver what she will have. The lesson, I think, is this: laugh at this character if you choose, satirize her to the nth National Lampoon Vacation sequel, but respect the currency with which she is abundantly endowed. She is coming to your city and she is coming to spend.

Notes

[1] Parts of this essay appear in my Introduction to *Daisy Miller* (Boston and New York: Bedford/St. Martins, 2013).

[2] Mark Twain (2002). *The Innocents Abroad*. Ed. Tom Quirk. New York: Penguin Books, 6, 7.

[3] For an account of the British Grand Tour tradition, see Jeremy Black (2003). James Buzard and William Stowe address the ways in which an early tourist industry successfully capitalizes on that tradition.

[4] Lynne Withey (1997). *Grand Tours and Cook's Tours: A History of Leisure Travel, 1750 to 1915*. New York: William Morrow, 61, 156.

[5] Mark Twain (2002). *The Innocents Abroad.* Ed. Tom Quirk. New York: Penguin Books, 13.

[6] Henry James (1974). *Henry James Letters: Volume I, 1843-75*. Ed. Leon Edel. Cambridge, MA. Harvard University Press, 152.

[7] Leon Edel (1962). *Henry James: The Conquest of London, 1870-1881*. Philadelphia: Lippincott, 302.

[8] James (1974), 152.

[9] Henry James (2013). *Daisy Miller: A Study*. Ed. William Merrill Decker. Boston: Bedford/St. Martins, 53. Further references to this edition will be included in the text.

[10] Peter Stoneley (2003) provides a variant perspective on the place of *Daisy Miller* in the emergence of the American girl heroine as a figure of popular fiction.

[11] Joseph F. Kett (1977). *Rites of Passage: Adolescence in America, 1790 to the Present*. New York: Basic, 168-171.

[12] Henry Adams (1983). *Democracy, Esther, Mont Saint Michel and Chartres, The Education of Henry Adams, Poems*. Eds. Ernest Samuels and Jayne N. Samuels. New York: Library of America, 802.
[13] *Ibid*.
[14] James (1974), 331.

Bibliography

Adams, Henry (1983). *Democracy, Esther, Mont Saint Michel and Chartres, The Education of Henry Adams, Poems*. Eds. Ernest Samuels and Jayne N. Samuels. New York: Library of America.

Black, Jeremy (2003). *The British Abroad: The Grand Tour in the Eighteenth Century*. London: The History Press.

Buzard, James (1993). *The Beaten Track: European Tourism, Literature, and the Ways to "Culture" 1800-1918*. Oxford: Clarendon.

Edel, Leon (1962). *Henry James: The Conquest of London, 1870-1881*. Philadelphia: Lippincott.

James, Henry (2013). *Daisy Miller: A Study*. Ed. William Merrill Decker. Boston: Bedford/St. Martins.

--- (1974). *Henry James Letters: Volume I, 1843-75*. Ed. Leon Edel. Cambridge, Massachusetts: Harvard University Press.

Kett, Joseph F. (1977). *Rites of Passage: Adolescence in America, 1790 to the Present*. New York: Basic.

Stoneley, Peter (2003). *Consumerism and American Girls' Literature, 1860-1940*. Cambridge, MA, and New York: Cambridge University Press.

Stowe, William (1994). *Going Abroad: European Travel in Nineteenth-Century American Culture*. Princeton: Princeton University Press.

Twain, Mark (2002). *The Innocents Abroad*. Ed. Tom Quirk. New York: Penguin Books.

Veblen, Thorstein (1931 [1899]). *The Theory of the Leisure Class: An Economic Study of Institutions*. New York: Modern Library.

Withey, Lynne (1997). *Grand Tours and Cook's Tours: A History of Leisure Travel, 1750 to 1915*. New York: William Morrow.

Simone Knewitz (Bonn)

'Try My Tivoli': Conspicuous Consumption in William Dean Howells's *A Modern Instance*

In the second half of the nineteenth century, a unified national mass market of consumer products began to emerge in the United States, turning Americans into purchasers of processed foods and packaged goods. Daniel Horowitz notes that "most antebellum Americans participated in a consumer economy." He also observes that "the shift from a producer to a consumer culture gained new momentum" between 1880 and 1920.[1] With the increasing competition between manufacturers on a national scale, producers began to devise new selling strategies to set apart their products from those of competitors. Brands like Heinz, Campbell's soup, or Quaker Oats were developed at the time, invented so that customers would establish personal relationships with the products and choose these brands over often identical, but unbranded alternatives.[2]

William Dean Howells's novel *A Modern Instance* (1882)[3] incorporates the emergent cultural phenomenon of product branding by associating its main protagonist, the journalist Bartley Hubbard, with a specific brand of beer.[4] Having settled his family in a respectable middle-class home in Boston, Hubbard indulges in his favorite beverage on a daily basis:

> He was rather particular about his beer, which he had sent in by the gross, – it came cheaper that way; after trying both the Cincinnati and the Milwaukee lagers, and making a cursory test of the Boston brand, he had settled down upon the American Tivoli; it was cheap, and you could drink a couple of bottles without feeling it. (185)

Howells does not invent an imaginary brand. Tivoli was an actually existing product made in Denver, Colorado, by the Tivoli Brewing Company since 1870. The beer thus does not merely emphasize the novel's verisimilitude. It also very concretely links the text to a contemporary consumer item. Settling for this particular brand of beer, the Tivoli assumes the role of a marker of Bartley's personality, and it notably sets him apart from the other characters in the novel and their drinking habits.[5] As Ben Graydon's attentive reading shows, the text does not merely use the beverage to associate Bartley with modern day consumerism but also carefully distinguishes between Bartley's and other characters' references to the brand. Whenever the text relates the position of the narrator or one of the other protagonists, for instance that of Bartley's wife Marcia, it refers to "Tivoli beer," (e.g., 275) using the brand name as a qualifying adjective. Relating Bartley's own thoughts or words, however, the novel omits the product category, and "Tivoli" stands in for the beer itself. "Successful product branding in Howells's time," Graydon suggests, "could be measured by the degree to which elements of the brand – most important, the product or company name – came to substitute in private discourse for the product category they were intended to suggest."[6] The fact that only Bartley uses this form marks his role as a modern-day consumer, setting him apart from the more conservative characters of the novel, like Marcia or the lawyer Atherton.[7]

Late nineteenth-century Victorian culture has often figured as an age of excess in the critical imagination, reflecting the new culture of abundance that emerged with the rise of industrial capitalism, the department store, and consumer credit.[8] Picturing literary realists like Henry James and William Dean Howells as oppositional to this emergent mass culture, some scholars have proposed that these authors eschewed the consumer culture of their time, instead projecting alternate visions of a democratic civil society in their novels.[9] Referring to realism's civilizatory project, Amy Kaplan thus suggests that the literary movement works from a " utopian impulse that strives to contribute to the formation of a new kind of public sphere, controlled neither by the traditions of an elite nor the dictates of the marketplace."[10] Simultaneously, however, Kaplan also urges us to see "realism's relation to social change not as a static background which novels either naively record or heroically evade, but as the foreground of the narrative structure of each novel."[11] Even more forcefully asserting the notion of literature as a cultural practice, Walter Benn Michaels criticizes any attempt by literary critics to define a dialectical relationship between the literary and the 'real,'[12] insisting to the contrary, as Michael Bell paraphrases Michaels, that "texts are not *responses* to [cultural] practices or [ideological] formations but *part* of them."[13]

Arguably, Michaels, by picturing literature as merely one of multiple cultural practices, downplays the specificity of literary discourse and its propensity to voice cultural critique. And yet, Howells's subtle incorporation of product branding in *A Modern Instance* does exemplify how works of literary realism, despite their ambivalences about consumerism, also participated in the logic of modern capitalist society, calling into question literature's alleged oppositional stance. In this sense, Mark McWilliams has explored Howells's text in the context of the new restaurant culture of the eighteen-seventies and -eighties, arguing that novels like *A Modern Instance* enabled their audience to make sense of the "restaurant as a new arena for public performance in American life," thus "chronicl[ing] the shifts in American eating habits but also help[ing] to encode these changes with social meaning."[14] Graydon's and McWilliams's interpretations give a sense of the processual nature of the social reality Howells and other realist authors constructed in their texts.

Expanding on their work, my present reading shows that despite the fact that *A Modern Instance* foregrounds a disavowal of commodity culture by associating consumption with excess, moral deterioration, and a decline of social institutions, its realist aesthetics ultimately cannot dispense with it either, as the novel needs to represent what it repudiates. Rather than in projecting a vision of an alternate, more democratic public sphere, the power of Howells's novel rests in its nuanced depiction of the then-emerging spectacular consumer culture. Reading *A Modern Instance* in the context of the social and economic developments of the time, I argue that representations of consumerism are central to Howells's negotiations of an altered public sphere. In the following, I will first use Thorstein Veblen's contemporaneous sociological theory of "conspicuous consumption" to analyze Howells's depiction of his main character Bartley Hubbard as an excessive consumer who lacks moral integrity and whose increasing physical and mental deterioration we witness. In a second section, exploring the role of newspapers as modern mass medium and the visual spectacle of the urban sphere, I show that Howells sees Bartley as a symptom of a modern culture, not merely as an aberration. Ultimately, Bartley and Marcia Hubbard appear as representatives of a rising modern American middle class of consumers.

1. "He was rather particular about his beer": Bartley Hubbard as Conspicuous Consumer

Published a decade and a half after *A Modern Instance*, Veblen's influential volume *The Theory of the Leisure Class* (1899) presents a critical response to modern capitalism. According to Veblen, the phenomenon of conspicuous consumption results from the differentiation of society into classes in a private property system that emphasizes the relationship between property and social status. Veblen identifies two primary ways for the upper class, which accumulates wealth by appropriating the surplus produced by the working class to confer their status in society: conspicuous leisure – the public display of leisure activities – and conspicuous consumption. The latter, Veblen argues, rises to particular prominence in modern mobile and urban societies. In contrast to smaller, rural communities where every inhabitant is well-informed about the activities of their neighbors, public images of consumption, instantaneously signaling social status, become more powerful in less tightly knit environments. Importantly, Veblen suggests that conspicuous consumption is not merely a phenomenon of the leisure class, but determines all consumer behavior. Attempting to raise their own social prestige, members of all social classes emulate consumer patterns of the next higher class, even if this effort stretches their own means of living. This results in a society determined by ever-changing processes of distinguishing oneself through the consumption of goods, as the specific tastes that are being emulated will vary according to particular social environments and are adaptable to technological and social advancement.[15]

Written at a time when socioeconomic changes in American society at once brought about a stricter stratification of classes and an erosion of traditional social hierarchies,[16] Howells's *A Modern Instance* introduces its main character Bartley Hubbard as a conspicuous consumer who shapes his own identity as well as his social status through public acts of consumption. The novel revolves around the romance, marriage, and eventual divorce of the couple Bartley Hubbard and Marcia Gaylord. Having eloped from Marcia's rural New England hometown by the name of Equity, they settle in Boston. Though Bartley had originally planned to pursue a career in law, he opts for journalism, choosing a profession that centers "on fleeting moments in the present" rather than one based on precedent.[17] His success in the field, however, is premised on opportunism and the sensationalism of his stories, and his moral deterioration is illustrated by his increasing consumption of beer, by his weight gain, and financial irresponsibility. Subsequently, he leaves Marcia and their baby behind in Boston and finally divorces her in an Indiana court; his life ends in a fatal shooting in Arizona; appropriately, an enraged citizen kills him on account of stories in his tabloid paper.

In the little rural town of Equity, Bartley stands out from the other citizens through his meticulous way of dressing himself. Though he is not rich by any measure, his demeanor suggests wealth. As Veblen notes, when it comes to signaling social status, "expenditure on dress has this advantage over most other methods, that our apparel is always in evidence and affords an indication of our pecuniary standing to all observers at first glance." Therefore, "people will undergo a very considerable degree of privation in the comforts or the necessaries of life in order to afford what is considered a decent amount of wasteful consumption" when it comes to dress.[18] This is certainly true of Bartley, who wears "his one suit as if it were but one of many" (14) and, in the manner of the Boston bourgeoisie, has his clothes made by a tailor instead of buying them mass-fabricated from a store (78).

Bartley clearly uses his way of dressing to project an image of prosperity that aims at what Veblen calls "invidious comparison"[19] with the rural population of Equity. His consumption is supposed to generate envy among the town's inhabitants, at once depreciating them as backwards and increasing his own self-worth. Early on, the text emphasizes the spectacular relationship between Hubbard and the townspeople by making Bartley the object of the stable-boy's admiration. Watching Bartley eat a piece of mince-pie in the middle of the night, Andy is at awe at the "splendor which showed itself in Mr. Hubbard's city-cut clothes, and in his neck-scarfs and the perfection of his finger-nails and mustache" (12) as well as his city-informed, modern eating habits: "Andy pulled his chair round so as to get an unrestricted view of a man who ate his pie with his fork as easily as another would with a knife" (12).[20] Focalized through Andy's perspective, making Bartley the object of his gaze, the passage presents consumption as a visual spectacle.

Simultaneously, Bartley's appearance causes uneasiness with the local committee that searches a new editor for the *Free Press*, the Equity newspaper. Men of humble origins themselves, the committee members "justly fear [...] the encroachments of hereditary aristocracy" (14) as they mistake Bartley's apparel for that of someone belonging to the bourgeois establishment:

> They perhaps had their misgivings when the young man, in his well-blacked boots, his gray trousers neatly fitting over them, and his diagonal coat buttoned high with one button, stood before them with his thumbs in his waistcoat pockets, and looked down over his mustache at the floor with sentiments concerning their wisdom which they could not explore; they must have resented the fashionable keeping of everything about him, for Bartley wore his one suit as if it were but one of many; but when they understood that he had come by everything through his own unaided smartness, they could no longer hesitate. (14)

The committee hires Bartley because they see a reflection of themselves in him, perceiving him as a self-made man in the tradition of Benjamin Franklin. Allegedly, Bartley has risen from poverty by his own intellectual faculties and hard work, having come to wealth by the productive labor of his own hands. However, Bartley's appearance deceives the committee, as they misrecognize his exquisite dress as a marker of his success, failing to understand that Bartley represents a new economy of spending which replaces an older model of productivity. The text does not portray Bartley as intentionally deceptive; indeed, he merely emulates his college friend Ben Halleck's richer lifestyle, who introduced him to "the splendors and elegances" of Boston social life, as well as to his tailor (18). As increasingly becomes clear as the novel progresses, his modern attention to surfaces implies a lack of character and moral integrity, diverging from Franklin's model.

The logic of conspicuous consumption also characterizes Bartley's courtship of and marriage to Marcia Gaylord. Initially, he is drawn to her exceptional beauty: "she had more style than any other girl" (13) and is comparatively better educated than other village girls. Bartley's attraction to his wife is premised on Marcia's "exhibition value."[21] He appears most fond of her when others admire her. Throughout the novel, Marcia is defined by a lack of agency. As Kimberly Freeman notes, "Marcia is continually described in terms of the image she impresses on others," and as a figure, she "both functions as a spectacle and is obsessed with spectacle."[22] First staying in a hotel in Boston, Marcia is intimidated by the "vastness of hotel mirrors and chandeliers, the glossy paint, the frescoing, the fluted pillars, the tessellated marble pavements" (101) of the establishment, and mortified at the thought of embarrassing herself and Bartley in public. Later on, disliking the spectacle of theaters, concerts, and restaurants, her social life remains tied to Bartley, whom she accompanies to public places because he wants her to go, but not because it gives her pleasure (128-129).

While living in Equity, Bartley attempts to cultivate the habitus of a person from the city, seeking to distinguish himself from the town's inhabitants. As he and Marcia arrive in Boston, people immediately identify Marcia and him as country people, as they fail to display the right urban habitus (101). Bartley's allegedly fashionable ways look provincial until he begins to cultivate Boston tastes, frequenting art museums and the opera. At first taking afternoon strolls in the Commons, "among the lovers whose passion had a publicity that neither surprised nor shocked them" (130), Bartley and Marcia soon resort to the more proper Public Garden as they realize the social stratification of public places.

"Consumption," Veblen suggests, "becomes a larger element in the standard of living in the city than in the country," as it becomes necessary to impress "transient observers, and to retain one's self-complacency under their observation."[23] Bartley's success as a newspaperman in Boston, then, is dependent on his mastering and performing urban lifestyle and fashion, and consumption plays a key role in the transformation of Bartley's social position. *A Modern Instance* links Bartley's and Marcia's visits to restaurants to their rise in social status. Initially dazzled by the spectacle of public eating in a humble restaurant and quite unsure about the appropriate behavior, Bartley and Marcia soon learn the art of conspicuous consumption, eating at places which are actually beyond their financial means:

> [T]hey went out and dined at Copeland's, or Weber's, or Fera's, or even at Parker's: they had long since forsaken the humble restaurant with its doilies and its ponderous crockery, and they had so mastered the art of ordering that they could manage a dinner as cheaply at these finer places as anywhere, especially if Marcia pretended not to care much for her half of the portion, and connived at its transfer to Bartley's plate. (130)

The social meaning of eating at a restaurant well surpasses the mere consumption of food. What matters is to be seen in fashionable establishments. As in the case of the Tivoli beer, Howells establishes a link to the culture of his readers, mentioning for instance one of Boston's famous restaurants, Parker's, which was the city's closest equivalent to New York's even more famous Delmonico's.[24] Bartley uses restaurants and the public life of the city to create calculated effects in order to impress out-of-town visitors such as his old friend Kinney, whom he takes to Parker's: "Bartley thought it well to concentrate as many dazzling effects upon him as he could in the single evening at his disposal" (223-224); or his father-in-law Squire Gaylord, who, however, appears to remain unmoved: "Bartley tried to impress him with such novel traits of cosmopolitan life as a *table d'hôte* dinner at a French restaurant; but the Squire sat through the courses, as if his barbarous old appetite had satisfied itself in that manner all his life" (172).

Incorporating the then-new social space of the restaurant, which "replaced the eating houses and taverns common through the middle of the nineteenth century,"[25] *A Modern Instance* traces some of the contemporary transformations of the cityscape which effected a shift between the private and the public and a new conception of the public sphere. As Mark McWilliams argues, novels like Howells's assumed an influential role in making readers familiar with these new kinds of dining establishments. He suggests that "[n]ovels [...] helped readers understand restaurants' strange mixture of public and private space: the best of the new establishments were places to be seen as well as places to dine."[26] The space of the restaurant brings a private aspect of life into public view and turns it into a form of public performance.

Of all characters, *A Modern Instance* most closely associates Bartley Hubbard with acts of consumerism, particularly with the consumption of food, drink, and expensive clothing. We encounter him eating mince-pie in the middle of the night in Equity (12), devour stewed kidneys and lyonnaise potatoes in his club (185), or frequent oyster-bars with his friend Ricker (188). Most importantly, references to Tivoli beer occur throughout the text, and the novel consistently links Bartley's drinking habit with the progressive degeneration of his character and his body, as the beer is also responsible for his steady weight gain. Thus, Bartley's consumption of food and drink leads to his physical deterioration and moral decline.

Bartley in fact welcomes this body fat, which he himself attributes to the beer, as a signifier of his affluence and solidity. Thus he asks Ricker to visit him at home "and try my Tivoli on Sunday. That's what gives a man girth" (220). The narrator, however, takes a more ironic perspective, associating the beer with Bartley's lack of morality: "He attributed the fat on his ribs to the Tivoli; perhaps it was also owing in some degree to a good conscience, which is a much easier thing to keep than people imagine" (186). While the first part of this sentence clearly takes Bartley's perspective, the last clause indicates a criticism of him, hinting at the fact that Bartley's physical solidity does precisely not equal moral integrity. Critique is also voiced through the perspective of Ricker, who explicitly connects Bartley's weight gain with degeneracy:

> But now, as he looked at Bartley's back, [...] it struck him as the back of a degenerate man, and that increasing bulk seemed not to represent an increase of wholesome substance, but a corky, buoyant tissue, materially responsive to some sort of moral dry-rot. (220)

In a moment of self-consciousness Bartley himself thinks that "he might be over-doing the beer; yes, he thought he must cut down on the Tivoli; he was getting ridiculously fat" (239). Yet this moment of self-doubt quickly vanishes, and when he leaves Marcia, he leaves behind unpaid bills "for indefinitely repeated dozens of Tivoli beer" (275).

As these examples attest, *A Modern Instance* associates consumption primarily with lack of integrity, excess, and degeneration. Bartley's indulgence in food and drink is paralleled by his excess in other areas of his life and by the fact that he lives according to an economy of spending. Despite his increased earnings, Bartley's spending accelerates at an even faster rate, to the point that he becomes indebted, and even begins to speculate and gamble with money borrowed from his friend Ben Halleck.[27] In contrast, his wife Marcia constantly seeks to economize, displaying a conservative relationship to money. The novel explicitly ties immorality and consumerism together when Bartley plagiarizes his friend Kinney's story, selling it to a rival newspaper, and uses the money to buy an expensive sacque for Marcia, and a sealskin cap for himself (229). When Marcia learns that Bartley gained the money for the purchase through an illegitimate transaction, she refuses to ever wear the garment again (231).

Andrew Trigg has suggested that Veblen's theory can be extended with Pierre Bourdieu's more differentiated framework, particularly with his notion of "cultural capital," referring to the way in which the leisure class uses its accumulated culture to distinguish themselves from people with 'new money.'[28] Cultural capital surpasses the mere accumulation of financial wealth, as it is acquired through education and social upbringing and hence only available to members of an established social elite. This elite must distinguish itself by taste from that which is popular. This distinction provides a more powerful way of exclusion than conspicuous consumption:

> The naïve exhibitionism of "conspicuous consumption," which seeks distinction in the crude display of ill-mastered luxury, is nothing compared to the unique capacity of the pure gaze, a quasi-creative power which sets the aesthete apart from the common herd by a radical difference which seems to be inscribed in "persons."[29]

A Modern Instance draws a distinction between Hubbard and the Halleck family, who represent the Boston Brahmin society. Bartley Hubbard is not 'new money,' like for instance the main protagonist of Howells's subsequent novel *The Rise of Silas Lapham* (1885), but represents the middle class.[30] Nevertheless, the text makes a point of differentiating between Bartley's habits of consumption and the refined tastes of the Hallecks, in whose life conspicuous consumption is conspicuously absent. The Hallecks certainly belong to the leisure class in the sense of Veblen's theory, but refuse to participate in the modern culture of spectacular consumption: they "were not fashionable people, but they lived wealthily" and "their house was richly furnished with cushioned seats, dense carpets, and heavy curtains; and they were visited by other people of their denomination, and of a like abundance" (18). The elder Mr. Halleck considers his family "plain people" (147) still living according to a doctrine of fashion of thirty years ago, which shows, for instance, in the fact that they do not live in the Back Bay neighborhood, but continue to stay in their now less fashionable house on Rumford Street, once the home of "solid citizens," but "now almost wholly abandoned to the boarding-houses of the poorer class" (148). This characterizes them as conservative, but it also ensures that the Hallecks are perceived as more refined. Yet, old-fashioned to the core, the Hallecks simultaneously appear as members of a class on the brink of obsolescence.

The novel presents consumption as a profoundly modern phenomenon that is instrumental in the larger shifts of social values in the contemporary culture, which works according to an economy of spending and of public display. Consumption's emphasis on surfaces and visual appearances replaces older notions of "character."[31] Howells's derogatory portrayal of consumerism thereby stands in an interesting tension to the discursive construction of the middle class in early nineteenth-century America in which performances of consumption were associated with feminine domesticity and true womanhood and signaled civility and virtuousness. As Lori Merish argues, "consumerism and its discourses established forms of political mediation through which feminine political subjectivities were defined, constituted, and contested." [32] In this vein, Katja Kanzler argues in her study of New England factory girl literature in this volume how representations of consumption helped to produce agency for working-class women. Howells's later text, centering on a male consumer, elucidates both the gendered dynamic of middle-class consumption in the U.S. cultural imaginary, which counters consumption deemed appropriate for women with masculine asceticism, [33] as well as literary realism's heightened anxiety about the culture of consumption in the second half of the nineteenth century.

2. The Commodification of Everyday Lives: Renegotiating the Public Sphere

As a "figure of modernity"[34] Bartley Hubbard is best described by his lack of character, i.e., a lack of moral integrity that is replaced by intelligence and opportunism. If the text portrays this as Bartley's individual failure, he, too, represents a shift in the relationship between the private and the public, which becomes most visible in the new newspaper culture that the novel incorporates.

A Modern Instance portrays a public sphere that has undergone fundamental alterations, which seem to reverberate even in the most backward pastoral places in the country. Thus, in Marcia's hometown, the rural town of Equity, which the narrator consistently describes as hopelessly old-fashioned, religion "had largely ceased to be a fact of spiritual experience" and instead "embraced and included the world" (16). Religious life here no longer provides spiritual and moral guidance and rather functions as a form of entertainment. While the novel situates the city, with its increasingly sensational public life, at the center, the fact that the erosion of traditions has arrived even in Equity attests to the profoundness and irreversibility of the changes. One of the novelties comes with the *Free*

Press, the town newspaper, founded by an ambitious local politician striving to bring Equity its due prestige (19). As the paper faces its financial demise from its inception, its board hires Bartley as editor and publisher, who turns the *Free Press* into an economic success:

> He modelled the newspaper upon the modern conception, through which the country press must cease to have any influence in public affairs, and each paper becomes little more than an open letter of neighborhood gossip. But while he filled his sheet with minute chronicles of the goings and comings of unimportant persons, and with all attainable particulars of the ordinary life of the different localities, he continued to make spicy hits at the Enemies of Equity in the late struggle, and kept the public spirit of the town alive. He had lately undertaken to make known its advantages as a summer resort, and had published a series of encomiums upon the beauty of its scenery and the healthfulness of its air and water, which it was believed would put it in a position of rivalry with some of the famous White Mountain places. He invited the enterprise of outside capital, and advocated a narrow-gauge road up the valley of the river through the Notch, so as to develop the picturesque advantages of that region. In all this, the color of mockery let the wise perceive that Bartley saw the joke and enjoyed it, and it deepened the popular impression of his smartness. (20)

David Mindich suggests that newspapers began to change significantly in the eighteen-thirties. In this period, the pennies first dissociated themselves formally from the political parties, pursuing a detached form of journalism. [35] Bartley's "modern conception" reflects this shift to nonpartisanship, which in the town of Equity comes half a century later than in urban centers. When the town leaders around Squire Gaylord install Hubbard as editor, they defer some of their power to the younger man, who keeps "the public spirit of the town alive" (20) by reverting to printing mostly gossip about Equity's inhabitants. This approach helps to sell papers, but Bartley also uses the *Free Press* to generate economic opportunities, commodifying the small town's assets as he attracts outside capital, both in the form of tourism and investment. He thus manages to increase Equity's prestige, but simultaneously reconfigures the town according to modern capitalist principles. The narrator does not criticize Bartley's enterprise directly. But he does point to Bartley's insincerity and ironic detachment. The criticism here is not directed at the economic transformations but at Bartley's individual opportunism.

In Boston, the new public sphere is marked by the emergence of an altered newspaper culture as well. And again, Bartley Hubbard is at the forefront. First writing for the conservative paper *Daily Chronicle-Abstract*, Bartley subsequently becomes the editor of the rising, more sensationalist *Events*. Increasingly interested in gossip, the press works to shift the boundaries between the public and the private, not least in the "Solid Men of Boston" series, in which Bartley portrays successful businessmen by emphasizing their personality and private circumstances, not their public achievements. As Bartley interviews the elder Mr. Halleck, the latter remarks at one point: "There's a good deal of talk about the intrusiveness of the newspapers; all I know is that they've never intruded upon me" (147). Bartley considers his interviewees as his "victims" (147); his business is the commodification of life stories. As in the other stories he pursues, what matters to Bartley is that he caters to his audiences' expectations, delivering them the stock narratives which they have already come to accept.

This sense of an increasing intrusiveness of the new mass media into the private sphere was a concern to many of Howells's contemporaries; Samuel Warren and Louis Brandeis, in their well-known article "The Right to Privacy" published in the *Harvard Law Review* in 1890, for instance criticized the new orientation of the media. They wrote:

> The press is overstepping in every direction the obvious bounds of propriety and of decency. Gossip is no longer the resource of the idle and the vicious, but has become a trade, which is pursued with industry as well as effrontery.[36]

Warren and Brandeis were not alone in predicting an erosion of social standards. At the time, Katherine Adams notes,

> [l]egal scholars, society columnists, politicians, and even amateur gardeners were publishing similar protests against the forces of invasion, exposure, and consumption that they, too, characterized as dangerous to both the individual and the culture at large.[37]

Portrayed as an essentially opportunistic character, Bartley Hubbard is a representative of the very type of modern mass media that Warren and Brandeis criticize. Meeting in a Boston oyster-house "of singular excellence" (188), Hubbard and his friend Ricker, the editor of the *Chronicle-*

Abstract, discuss their respective moral outlooks on the role of the press. Ricker considers the newspaper a "great moral engine" which "ought to be run in the interest of the engineer" (189). To him,

> a newspaper [is] a public enterprise, with certain distinct duties to the public. It's sacredly bound not to do anything to deprave or debauch its readers; and it's sacredly bound not to mislead or betray them, not merely as to questions of morals and politics, but as to questions of what we lump as 'advertising.' (190)

If Ricker takes an idealist position, Bartley considers a newspaper first of all a commodity to be sold; he sees it as a private enterprise to make money that therefore should cater to the public's desires. In his work for the *Events*, he manages to transform the paper in an economically successful way that is "perfectly horrid" (167) to conservatives, with contents "full of murders and all uncleanness" (167).

As Kaplan explains, newspapers, though already circulating as mass media since the eighteen-thirties, only began to operate on a national level in the eighteen-eighties, emerging as a rival to literary realism's project to construct a public sphere.[38] The expansion of newspapers was directly linked to the rise of the department store and the marketing of manufactured brand-name goods, which prompted an accelerated demand for advertising space, as well as increased revenue generated through advertisements. A paper's worth, then, increasingly derived from its circulation, which determined its value as an advertising medium.[39] "This change," Kaplan observes,

> meant that the newspaper had to become a kind of advertisement for itself; if the paper's primary goal was to increase circulation in order to sell more products for its advertisers, it had to present the news in such ways as to advertise itself as a desirable product.[40]

Representing a broader social trend rather than a mere moral deviation, Hubbard's commitment to "spice" (192), Kaplan argues, "can be seen as a direct threat to Howells's conception of realism."[41] Like realism, mass-mediated journalism seeks to establish a public sphere, but it does so committed to the logic of the market and to consumption rather than to democratic social institutions.

3. Literary Realism, Conspicuous Consumption, and the Rise of the Middle Class

In *A Modern Instance*, depictions of conspicuous consumption serve to inscribe Bartley as a protagonist who possesses "personality" rather than "character," portraying his moral failure as individual deviance. His degeneracy, however, appears to be premised exclusively on his excessive acts of consumption. As nineteenth-century reviewer John M. Robertson aptly put it: "We vaguely feel, somehow, that Bartley would have prospered, with his unscrupulous views about journalism, if he had not got fat, and that then he would not have left his wife."[42] Howells's demonization of Hubbard's consumerism attests to his own ambivalence and may also signal a crisis in his own brand of realism. Warren Hedges argues that Howells's project is premised on the "claim to present the real disinterestedly," which involves the attempt "to arrive at representation free from desire."[43] Bartley, in contrast, "functions as an icon for everything that bourgeois and especially professional men are supposed to carry under erasure – embodiment, libidinous indulgence, and opportunistic self-interest."[44] His journalism caters to the desires that the realist work disavows in its attempt to portray society as a whole, yet that it cannot dispense with either.[45]

Referring to Howells's subsequent novel, Michaels suggests that "nothing is more remarkable in *The Rise of Silas Lapham* than the identification of realism with a morality and an economy that are themselves represented in principle as anticapitalist."[46] This statement also rings true for *A Modern Instance*. Howells projects a critical image of modernity and the new culture of consumption; however, as he describes processes which are only emerging, his text not merely records social changes, but also participates in the construction of the modern culture he describes. Phenomena like product branding and the new social space of the restaurant were only coming into being at the time Howells wrote his novel. In that sense, Howells's text also encodes these changes with social meaning. By including such images of urban spectacle, *A Modern Instance* also foreshadows some of the aspects that would rise to more prominence in the literature of the first decades of the twentieth century such as, for instance, Theodore Dreiser's novels.

To the extent that Howells traces new social trends and developments, meanwhile also rejecting the obsolete morality of the bourgeois establishment, the novel's power ultimately rests in the way it registers anxieties about the modern, in its portrayal of that which it ostensibly repudiates. It is possible to read Marcia and Bartley as representatives of an emerging new American middle class grounded in consumer culture and oblivious of previously existing class boundaries. The following passage describes the spectacle of Bartley and Marcia Hubbard walking their baby daughter Flavia in the streets of Boston:

> When the spring opened, Bartley pushed Flavia about the sunny pavements in a baby carriage, while Marcia paced alongside, looking under the calash top from time to time, arranging the bright afghan, and twitching the little one's lace hood into place. They never noticed that other perambulators were pushed by Irish nurse-girls or French bonnes; they had paid somewhat more than they ought for theirs, and they were proud of it merely as a piece of property. It was rather Bartley's ideal, as it is that of most young American fathers, to go out with his wife and baby in that way; he liked to have his friends see him; and he went out every afternoon he could spare. (176)

This passage from the novel's center provides the reader with an image of an American middle-class nuclear family publicly displaying their domestic life. While on the one hand, the narrator attributes the couple with naiveté – they have overpaid for their baby carriage and they fail to notice the class difference to the other children being promenaded in the streets –, on the other hand, it seems to be precisely their inability to apprehend these social nuances that makes them rightly American. The last sentence seems to foreshadow that the public, consumer-oriented performance of one's private identity may exactly be the coming modern American way of life.

Notes

[1] Daniel Horowitz (1985). *The Morality of Spending: Attitudes toward the Consumer Society in America, 1875-1940.* Baltimore: Johns Hopkins University Press, xxvi.

[2] See, e.g., Nancy F. Koehn (1999). "Henry Heinz and Brand Creation in the Late

Nineteenth Century: Making Markets for Processed Food." *Business History Review* 73.3, 349-352. On the invention of the modern mass market, see: Strasser (1989). On early developments of brand-name advertising, see Laird (1998), 31-37; as well as Norris (1990).
[3] William Dean Howells (2008 [1882]). *A Modern Instance.* Mineola, NY: Dover. Further references to this edition will be included in the text.
[4] Ben Graydon (2007). "Product Branding in Howells's *A Modern Instance." ANQ* 20.2, 36 (35-38).
[5] *Ibid.*
[6] *Ibid.*, 37.
[7] *Ibid.*
[8] See, e.g., Horowitz (1985).
[9] See, e.g., Winfried Fluck (1997). *Das kulturelle Imaginäre: Eine Funktionsgeschichte des amerikanischen Romans 1790-1900.* Frankfurt a. M.: Suhrkamp.
[10] Amy Kaplan (1988). *The Social Construction of American Realism.* Chicago: University of Chicago Press, 25.
[11] *Ibid.*, 9.
[12] Walter Benn Michaels (1987). *The Gold Standard and the Logic of Naturalism: American Literature at the Turn of the Century.* Berkeley: University of California Press.
[13] Michael Davitt Bell (1993). *The Problem of American Realism: Studies in the Cultural History of a Literary Idea.* Chicago: University of Chicago Press, 3 (emphasis in the text).
[14] Mark McWilliams (2009). "Conspicuous Consumption: Howells, James, and the Gilded Age Restaurant." *Culinary Aesthetics and Practices in Nineteenth-Century American Literature.* Eds. Monika M. Elbert and Marie Drews. New York: Palgrave Macmillan, 44.
[15] Thorstein Veblen (1994 [1899]). *The Theory of the Leisure Class.* Mineola, NY: Dover, see especially 1-70.
[16] Susan Goodman (2003). *Civil Wars: American Novelists and Manners, 1880-1940.* Baltimore: Johns Hopkins University Press, 16.
[17] Brook Thomas (1997). *American Literary Realism and the Failed Promise of Contract.* Berkeley: University of California Press, 25.
[18] Veblen (1994 [1899]), 103.
[19] *Ibid.*, 22.
[20] On the significance of mince-pie in *A Modern Instance*, see McWilliams (2009) as well as Porte (1985).
[21] I am here appropriating Walter Benjamin's term which he employs in his seminal essay "The Work of Art in the Age of Mechanical Production" to denote an artwork's value as a commodity (as opposed to its "cult value" or internal value). See Benjamin (1969 [1936]), 225. Transferred to the novel discussed here, "exhibition value" reflects Bartley's appreciation of Marcia as an asset by which he

seeks to increase his own social or cultural capital. Her value to him is determined by the heightened social prestige their relationship promises.

[22] Kimberley Freeman (2003). *Love American Style: Divorce and the American Novel, 1881-1976.* New York: Routledge, 44.

[23] Veblen (1994 [1899]), 55, 54.

[24] McWilliams (2009), 47.

[25] *Ibid.*, 36.

[26] *Ibid.*

[27] Walter Benn Michaels notes with reference to *The Rise of Silas Lapham* that Howells saw speculation "as the quintessentially capitalist gesture": Michaels (1987), 40.

[28] Andrew B. Trigg (2001). "Veblen, Bourdieu, and Conspicuous Consumption." *Journal of Economic Issues* 35.1, 104 (99-115).

[29] Pierre Bourdieu (1984). *Distinction.* London: Routledge, 23.

[30] For a Bourdeuian discussion of Silas Lapham see Barrish (2001), 23-30.

[31] Susman famously analyzes the shift in social psychology at the turn of the twentieth century: a transition from "character" to "personality" in the conceptionalization of selfhood and the presentation of the self in society. See Susman (1979), 212-226.

[32] Lori Merish (2000). *Sentimental Materialism: Gender, Commodity Culture, and Nineteenth-Century American Literature.* Durham: Duke University Press, 13.

[33] *Ibid.*, 73.

[34] Thomas (1997), 25.

[35] David Mindich (1998). *Just the Facts: How "Objectivity" Came to Define American Journalism.* New York: New York University Press, 12.

[36] Samuel Warren and Louis Brandeis (1890). "The Right to Privacy." *Harvard Law Review* 4.5, 196 (193-220).

[37] Katherine Adams (2009). *Owning Up: Privacy, Property, and Belonging in U.S. Women's Life Writing.* New York: Oxford University Press, 4.

[38] Kaplan (1988), 25-26.

[39] Michael Shudson (1978). *Discovering the News: A Social History of American Newspapers.* New York: Basic Books, 93.

[40] Kaplan (1988), 27-28.

[41] *Ibid.*, 30.

[42] Qtd. in: George Perkins (1974). "*A Modern Instance*: Howells' Transition to Artistic Maturity." *New England Quarterly* 47.3, 432 (427-439). A number of critics have commented that Bartley's deterioration over the course of the novel hardly seems credible. See, e.g., Tavernier-Courbin (1978).

[43] Warren Hedges (1996). "Howells's 'Wretched Fetishes': Character, Realism, and Other Modern Instances." *Texas Studies in Literature and Language* 38.1, 41 (26-50).

[44] *Ibid.*, 37.
[45] *Ibid.*, 42.
[46] Michaels (1987), 38.

Bibliography

Adams, Katherine (2009). *Owning Up: Privacy, Property, and Belonging in U.S. Women's Life Writing.* New York: Oxford University Press.

Bell, Michael Davitt (1993). *The Problem of American Realism: Studies in the Cultural History of a Literary Idea.* Chicago: University of Chicago Press.

Benjamin, Walter (1969 [1936]). "The Work of Art in the Age of Mechanical Reproduction." *Illuminations: Essays and Reflections.* New York: Schocken, 217-251.

Barrish, Phillip (2001). *American Literary Realism, Critical Theory, and Intellectual Prestige, 1880-1995.* Cambridge: Cambridge University Press.

Bourdieu, Pierre (1984). *Distinction*. London: Routledge.

Fluck, Winfried (1997). *Das kulturelle Imaginäre: Eine Funktionsgeschichte des amerikanischen Romans 1790-1900.* Frankfurt a. M.: Suhrkamp.

Freeman, Kimberly (2003). *Love American Style: Divorce and the American Novel, 1881-1976.* New York: Routledge.

Graydon, Ben (2007). "Product Branding in Howells's *A Modern Instance*." *ANQ* 20.2, 35-38.

Goodman, Susan (2003). *Civil Wars: American Novelists and Manners, 1880-1940.* Baltimore: Johns Hopkins University Press.

Hedges, Warren (1996). "Howells's 'Wretched Fetishes': Character, Realism, and Other Modern Instances." *Texas Studies in Literature and Language* 38.1, 26-50.

Horowitz, Daniel (1985). *The Morality of Spending: Attitudes toward the Consumer Society in America, 1875-1940.* Baltimore: Johns Hopkins University Press.

Howells, William Dean (2008 [1882]). *A Modern Instance*. Mineola, NY: Dover.

Kaplan, Amy (1988). *The Social Construction of American Realism*. Chicago: University of Chicago Press.

Koehn, Nancy F. (1999). "Henry Heinz and Brand Creation in the Late Nineteenth Century." *Business History Review* 73.3, 349-393.

Laird, Pamela Walter (1998). *Advertising Progress: American Business and the Rise of Consumer Marketing.* Baltimore: Johns Hopkins University Press.

McWilliams, Mark (2009). "Conspicuous Consumption: Howells, James, and the Gilded Age Restaurant." *Culinary Aesthetics and Practices in Nineteenth-Century American Literature*. Eds. Monika M. Elbert and Marie Drews. New York: Palgrave Macmillan, 35-52.

Merish, Lori (2000). *Sentimental Materialism: Gender, Commodity Culture, and Nineteenth-Century American Literature.* Durham: Duke University Press.

Michaels, Walter Benn (1987). *The Gold Standard and the Logic of Naturalism: American Literature at the Turn of the Century.* Berkeley: University of California Press.

Mindich, David (1998). *Just the Facts: How "Objectivity" Came to Define American Journalism.* New York: New York University Press.

Norris, James D. (1990). *Advertising and the Transformation of American Society, 1865-1920.* New York: Greenwood.

Perkins, George (1974). "*A Modern Instance*: Howells' Transition to Artistic Maturity." *New England Quarterly* 47.3, 427-439.

Porte, Joel (1985). "Manners, Morals, and Mince-Pie: Howells' America Revisited." *Prospects* 10, 443-460.

Shudson, Michael (1978). *Discovering the News: A Social History of American Newspapers.* New York: Basic Books.

Strasser, Susan (1989). *Satisfaction Guaranteed: The Making of the American Mass Market.* Washington: Smithsonian.

Susman, Warren (1979). "'Personality' and Twentieth-Century Culture." *New Directions in American Intellectual History.* Eds. John Higham and Paul K. Conkin. Baltimore: Johns Hopkins University Press, 212-226.

Tavernier-Courbin, Jacqueline (1978). "Towards the City: Howells' Characterization in *A Modern Instance.*" *Modern Fiction Studies* 24.1, 111-127.

Thomas, Brook (1997). *American Literary Realism and the Failed Promise of Contract.* Berkeley: University of California Press.

Trigg, Andrew B. (2001). "Veblen, Bourdieu, and Conspicuous Consumption." *Journal of Economic Issues* 35.1, 99-115.

Veblen, Thorstein (1994 [1899]). *The Theory of the Leisure Class.* Mineola, NY: Dover.

Warren, Samuel, and Louis Brandeis (1890). "The Right to Privacy." *Harvard Law Review* 4.5, 193-220.

Eva Boesenberg (Berlin)

Sex and the City: Gender and Consumption in Late Nineteenth-Century Fiction

My title establishes a connection between the well-known television series and three novels published around 1900. There is more to this relationship than the fact that the series self-consciously references Theodore Dreiser's *Sister Carrie* through the name of its central character. Rather, I will argue, the realist and naturalist narratives, like *Sex and the City*, portray urban spaces as sites where female characters encounter unprecedented opportunities to consume not only material things, but men as well. While such "purchasing possibilities," as Jennifer Scanlon calls them,[1] reshape the established gender order in significant ways, they paradoxically do not liberate these characters from being themselves perceived as objects. Their ability to consume remains premised on their performance as attractive spectacles for the male gaze.

In the following, I analyze this connection in three specific texts: Theodore Dreiser's *Sister Carrie* (1900), Paul Laurence Dunbar's *The Sport of the Gods* (1902), and Edith Wharton's *The Custom of the Country* (1913). While Dreiser's and Wharton's novels are exemplars of naturalist and realist fiction, Dunbar's narrative, which I suggest should also be considered as naturalist, adds interesting facets to the question of consumption because it draws attention to its racial as well as gender dimensions.

1. Erotics of Consumption in *Sister Carrie*

Carrie Meeber, the protagonist of the novel, already encounters the city as a space of consumption on her way to Chicago. It assumes the figure of Charles Drouet, a traveling salesman linked to stores whose wares she has coveted in the past. Carrie's own wages cannot gain her access to the plenty of the city in a way she finds satisfactory. Only by becoming

Drouet's mistress or, to put it less judgmentally, common law wife, does she attain what has been termed "consumer citizenship."[2]

Drouet's courting of her, which revolves around acts of consumption – of a good meal, but perhaps most importantly, the purchase of new clothing – both reflects and contributes to what Rachel Bowlby has described as consumer culture's model of female seduction.[3] In the text, this is acted out primarily in the newly established department stores, which are described in the following manner:

> They were along the line of the most effective retail organisation, with hundreds of stores coordinated into one and laid out upon the most imposing and economic basis. They were handsome, bustling, successful affairs, with a host of clerks and a swarm of patrons. Carrie passed along the busy aisles, much affected by the remarkable display of trinkets, dress goods, stationary, and jewelry. Each separate counter was a showplace of dazzling interest and attraction. She could not help feeling the claim of each trinket and valuable upon her personally, and yet she did not stop. There was nothing here which she could not have used – nothing which she did not long to own. The dainty slippers and stockings, the delicately frilled skirts and petticoats, the laces, ribbons, hair-combs, all touched her with individual desire, and she felt keenly the fact that not any of these things were in the range of her purchase.[4]

Whereas the department stores emerge as active presences in this passage, their importance underscored by anaphoric constructions ("they were"), Carrie, despite her movement, appears passive ("much affected," "could not help"), her own desire the result of being "touched" by the merchandise on display. The emotional quality of her response to the commodities is heightened by the shift to free indirect discourse and emphasized by the penultimate sentence's double negations repeated, for good measure, in anaphoric fashion. Alliteration and contrast contribute to the passage's strong rhythm. Above all, the detailed, expansive, almost fetishistic enumeration of goods suggests that the narrative voice's investment in consumption all but matches the central character's.

Based on what Walter Benjamin has called "the sex appeal of the inorganic,"[5] an intimate relationship is established between the consumer goods and the female customer. But Carrie's engagement with these objects is not limited to nonverbal communication. In some of the text's most memorable scenes, they address her in direct speech:

> Fine clothes to her were a vast persuasion; they spoke tenderly and Jesuitically for themselves. When she came within earshot of their pleading, desire in her bent a willing ear. [...] "My dear," said the lace collar she secured from Partridge's, "I fit you beautifully; don't give me up." "Ah, such little feet," said the leather of the soft new shoes; "how effectively I cover them. What a pity they should ever want my aid." (75)

In this scenario, Bärbel Tischleder remarks, "[t]hings assume the subject position."[6] Commodities become so central to people's sense of self in the city, Philip Fisher argues, that the characters "seek to be absorbed temporarily into the magical life of the things."[7]

The "sexual culture of the department store," as Gail Reekie terms it, is clearly gendered. These new shopping institutions "created modern manhood and womanhood," according to Reekie, and as "heterosexual spaces" shaped how "women and men viewed and related to each other as sexes."[8] Frequently, the interaction between 'active' male sales managers and 'passive' female consumers was described through analogies to courtship. This did not mean that men were exempt from being judged on the basis of their consumer choices. Like the female characters, Drouet and Hurstwood are socially positioned on the basis of their clothing. The novel devotes extensive passages to descriptions of their sartorial styles (3, 33). Like the narrator, Carrie immediately deduces Hurstwood's superiority from the contrast between the patent leather of Drouet's shoes and the "soft, black calf, polished only to a dull shine" of the older man's (73).

And yet, except for Drouet's initial clothing of Carrie in new garb which, as Irene Gammel suggests, "acts as a kind of foreplay,"[9] men are hardly ever seen shopping in *Sister Carrie*. 'Manly' consumption takes place primarily in restaurants and bars. Surrounded by "brightly coloured tiles, […] rich, dark, polished wood, which reflected the light, and coloured stucco-work, which gave the place a very sumptuous appearance" (33), in the company of "politicians, brokers, actors, […] [and] rich 'rounders' of the town" (32), Drouet can express his aspirations to a higher social position by consuming pricey food and drinks.

For Carrie, yet another locus of consumption turns out to be crucial, one that offers not material things but entertainment: the theater. It is this institution that allows Carrie to become wealthy and famous, ending her economic dependence on men. As Jennifer Brezina points out, acting became a respectable profession in the late nineteenth century. Actresses were no longer automatically associated with prostitution. Even though

Carrie's performance on stage reflects hegemonic gender discourses, Brezina argues, the fact that this version of 'true womanhood' is explicitly presented as a *performance* may have a deconstructive effect. By "emphasizing the artificiality of the feminine," Brezina notes, women are able to "wield a certain type of destabilizing power. By 'acting' their identities as though they were roles in a play, women undermine the essentialist notions of gender divisions and stereotypes."[10]The control over financial capital acquired through turning the usually unremunerated labor of representation into gainful employment further recalibrates the gendered balance of power.

Eventually, Carrie's sizeable income, but even more so her *credit* offer access to seemingly unlimited consumption, identified with the city as a whole and even with "the world" (334). Her consumer choices extend to include a selection of potential male love objects: "Without money – or the requisite sum, at least – she enjoyed the luxuries which money could buy. [...] Men sent flowers, love notes, offers of fortune" (334).

While her former partner Hurstwood commits suicide after his financial and corporeal resources have been expended in what has been termed naturalism's 'plot of exhaustion' or 'plot of decline,' Carrie's rise intersects with it to form the novel's x-shaped plot. Even though she has two lovers, neither of whom she is legally married to, she escapes inscription in the 'fallen woman' paradigm the text lays out for her at the very beginning:

> When a girl leaves her home at eighteen, she does one of two things. Either she falls into saving hands and becomes better, or she rapidly assumes the cosmopolitan standard of virtue and becomes worse. Of an intermediate balance, under circumstances, there is no possibility. (1)

Despite the finality of the phrasing, Carrie's development in fact complicates this dichotomy in one of the text's most productive revisions of nineteenth-century hegemonic gender discourses. The fact that Carrie to some extent elides the wife/prostitute binarism might be related to the transfer of libidinal charges from men to material goods. She is portrayed as curiously asexual. Her emotions are primarily invested in the consumption of clothes, the fetishization of money, and her career as an actress. These turn out to be intimately connected:

> […] when Carrie heard Drouet's laudatory opinion of her dramatic ability, her body tingled with satisfaction. […] It was a delightful sensation while it lasted. […] It was as if he had put fifty cents in her hand and she had exercised the thoughts of a thousand dollars. (117-118)

Such an almost orgasmic response to praise from a male viewer, which the text only registers in the context of the theater, can be read as acquiescence in her position as a 'mirror' of the male gaze, which perhaps made her triumph more palatable for a contemporary audience. Through the simile, the passage links Carrie's enjoyment of praise to her eroticization of money, which the narrative voice notes in several other instances as well.

Instead of branding her as materialist, however, the text represents her response as an exertion of her imaginative faculties, a creative activity: "[…] her dreams ran riot. The one hundred and fifty! the one hundred and fifty! What a door to an Aladdin's cave it seemed to be. […] She conceived of delights which were not – saw lights of joy that never were on land or sea" (334). Finally, Carrie's success is rendered less threatening by being attributed not to any initiative, let alone ambition on her part, but to chance and her ability to seize opportunities that present themselves to her.

In typical naturalist fashion, she is also subjected to the narrator's condescension for much of the text, beginning with an implicit criticism of her poor consumer choices ("cheap imitation alligator-skin satchel," 1) in the novel's very first sentence. Somewhat implausibly, Carrie's passion for consumption is finally transformed into artistic aspiration. She considers performing in 'serious' plays, rather than the melodramas in which she has starred so far. At the end of the text, she is explicitly denied happiness, as well as romantic love. Yet even so, she has significantly revised the gendered status quo, not least through her position as both the subject and an object of consumption. While this might also be said of Kitty Hamilton, a central character in *The Sport of the Gods*, Dunbar's novel judges such behavior quite differently.

2. Consumption as the Loss of Moral Capital in *The Sport of the Gods*

Dunbar's Harlem shares many of the features associated with Chicago and Manhattan's Upper West Side (78th Street and Amsterdam Avenue) in *Sister Carrie*. Yet these urban spaces are perceived from differently racialized perspectives, which results in contrasting accentuations of the female characters' engagements with the emergent consumer society. Unlike Carrie, the Hamiltons do not leave their small-town home voluntarily; rather, they have to flee the South after the father, Berry Hamilton, has been imprisoned for a theft he did not commit. His lawyer's plea for his innocence, no matter how well founded, cannot prevail against racist assumptions that a black man accused of a crime must be guilty.

Berry Hamilton's sentence destroys the family's respectability and deprives them of their home, their occupations, and their standing in the local communities, proving the South to be "an uninhabitable symbolic geography for the black population," as Lawrence R. Rodgers argues.[11] Through their move North, they hope to escape post-bellum socio-economic relations still rooted, as Houston A. Baker suggests, in an economics of slavery.[12]

In New York, the Hamiltons soon realize that their new social environment operates according to rules of distinction that differ from those of their home town. Where upward social mobility had earlier been based on *saving*, the city requires *spending*, especially on clothes and entertainment. In the case of the son, such consumption is again focused on a bar. But Joe does not only, like Drouet, go to "The Banner" to spend some of his hard-earned money on food, drink, and the company of other men. Becoming addicted to alcohol and losing his position as a barber, he metamorphoses into one of the "well-dressed idlers" who turn their presence at the bar into a livelihood, relying on others to buy them food and drinks. In effect, he exchanges a symbolic resource one might, following S. M. Miller's and Anthony J. Savoie's Respect and Rights, describe as a form of social capital[13] – the respect he and the other regulars pay their benefactors – for alimentation.

The text censors Joe's conduct not only because it violates the principle of honesty. The spenders are tricked into paying by the Banner's "fraternity" of con-men. It further takes issue with Joe since he eschews the values of hegemonic masculinity: the Protestant work ethic, economic self-reliance, and capital accumulation. He forfeits his manhood not merely because he shuns the responsibility of labor and provisioning but also because, like Hurstwood, he earns his livelihood by way of representation, an existence conventionally associated with femininity.

Joe's symbolic loss of manhood is intertwined with his relationship to an actress, Hattie Sterling. Having corrupted him by initiating him into the ways of the city, she nevertheless tries to steer him back to sobriety and steady employment.[14] Yet when he is transformed into "Frankenstein" (197) and kills her in a drunken rage, her fate is represented as self-inflicted. The monster metaphor suggests that it is her own creature that proves her undoing (208-209).

In contradistinction to the narrator of Dreiser's novel, the narrative voice in *The Sport of the Gods* roundly condemns the theater on moral grounds. The text registers the opportunities it provides for women in terms of income and self-determination, but refuses to credit them. This becomes most clearly visible in the case of Joe's sister Kitty, who follows in Hattie Sterling's footsteps. She parlays her talent as a singer and performer, as well as her erotic capital, into financial self-reliance rather than marriage. If her mother still regards a woman's virginity as her capital and death as preferable to the loss of virtue signified by scant apparel, Kitty rightly argues that "'nowadays everybody thinks stage people respectable up here'" (167, 166). At a time when there were few employment options for black women outside of the domestic sector, acting, or entertainment more generally, provided its practitioners with financial rewards and a degree of self-determination hardly equaled elsewhere.

Because the songs she has to present rely on racist clichés, Rodgers maintains, her new profession represents no advance over her previous situation: "Kitty is transformed from a stock southern plantation figure into the novel's minstrel re-enactment of the same emblem. She leaves one racist code of behavior to become engulfed in another."[15] But the argument Brezina advances perhaps applies here as well. Performing a stereotyped version of 'black femininity' on stage for a limited amount of time might be less demeaning than being forced to perform it outside of the theater for less recognition and much lower financial returns.

The narrative voice refuses to acknowledge anything of value in Kitty's career – which strikingly resembles Carrie's –, describing the actress as all surface and social ambition: "From the time that she went on the stage she had begun to live her own life, a life in which the chief aim was the possession of good clothes and the ability to attract the attention which she had learned to crave" (216). The persistent moralism in which Kitty Hamilton's lifestyle is likened to her brother's (who, after all, ends up a murderer) suggests an ethical double standard that functions to obscure Kitty's rather striking upward social and economic mobility. The stature she manages to achieve despite her dual marginalization would seem to command respect from any vantage point other than her mother's and the narrative voice's unrelenting code of righteousness.

A number of factors contribute to these contrasting evaluations of acting in Dreiser's and Dunbar's narratives. *The Sport of the Gods*, first, focuses on the loss of manhood racism entails, which relegates the female characters to the margins. It also draws a much more negative image of city life as a whole. Part of this might be due to the role of respectability in African Americans' fight for civil rights around 1900, specifically the idea of "black uplift" propagated, among other organizations, by the African American women's club movement.[16] Many Americans of African descent identified stereotypes of black sexual permissiveness as powerful rhetorical tools that contributed to an entrenchment of white supremacy.[17] A desire to distance oneself as comprehensively as possible from such discourses is recognizable in the construction of Kitty Hamilton.

Further, earlier texts by black writers such as Frances Ellen Watkins Harper's *Iola Leroy* (1892) argued that, as a group, African Americans might contribute to the development of the United States through their moral capital. Derived from unearned "pain and suffering" that generated "gold more fine than the pavements of heaven,"[18] such assets might complement the "nation's building up a great material prosperity, founding magnificent cities, grasping the commerce of the world, or excelling in literature, art, and science."[19] African American religiosity and moral superiority, in other words, might temper the rampant materialism of the Gilded Age. There are echoes of such reasoning in the fashion *The Sport of the Gods*' depicts Berry Hamilton. And yet, Dunbar's assessment of the likelihood that such a gift might be valued is much more pessimistic than Harper's, reflecting the political changes between the publication dates of the two books – 1892 and 1902 –, the political rollback after the end of Reconstruction and the installment of Jim Crow legislation in the U.S. American South in particular.

In Dunbar's novel, New York City remains a space inimical to black progress. Berry and Fannie Hamilton return to their former home rather than endure its corrupting influence. This is a striking assessment of an urban environment well known for the 'Harlem Renaissance' that emerged a mere two decades, by some counts only a few years later.[20] But the rural South is no more conducive to black progress than the Northern cityscape; the Hamiltons live out their remaining days in resignation (255). At a time that has been described as the nadir of U.S. American race relations after the end of slavery, neither consumption nor productive labor or the demonstration of sterling morality can gain them full citizenship.

3. Consuming Men, Challenging *The Custom of the Country*

Like the other two novels discussed, Edith Wharton's text portrays New York, in this case the Upper West Side, Fifth Avenue, and Washington Square, as a site of conspicuous consumption. But in a version of the 'international theme,' protagonist Undine Spragg extends her shopping tours to Europe, especially the French capital, a consumer's paradise:

> Her senses luxuriated in all its material details: the thronging motors, the brilliant shops, the novelty and daring of the women's dresses, the piled-up colours of the ambulant flower-carts, the appetizing expanse of the fruiterers' windows, even the chromatic effects of the *petits fours* behind the plate-glass of the pastry-cooks: all the surface-sparkle and variety of the inexhaustible streets of Paris.[21]

Undine's attention to detail and her progressive immersion in the experience of window-shopping are conveyed by the increasing length of the syntactic elements in this enumeration, with the genitive constructions signaling an ever more sophisticated appreciation of the wares displayed. Despite the centrality of food in this tableau, though, Undine's consumption is primarily visual, the spectacle of luxury made available yet contained by the plate-glass windows of the establishments she passes. What she covets are not only Parisian sartorial fashions and entertainment but also European men, specifically those who command a precious form of social capital, an aristocratic title. Throughout, she seeks to achieve upward social mobility by marrying partners of ever higher social standing. This is made possible by three major factors: her looks, her father's financial capital, and the increasing acceptability of divorce.

As the novel opens, Undine is investing heavily in her physical appearance, as well as her social skills, with a view towards attracting a spouse from New York's social elite. Drawing on her father's money, she spends lavishly not only on sumptuous attire but also on markers of status, such as a box at the opera, which she deems indispensable for conveying the 'right' kind of impression to the 'right' kind of people. At the same time, she eagerly studies social distinctions, implementing her new-found knowledge by presenting herself in a more elegant manner. It is Undine's singular talent for embodying grandeur, her spectacular specular capacity, that constitutes her greatest asset. Always adjusting her sartorial, gestural, verbal, and vocal self-presentation to what she perceives as the most prestigious style, she continually enhances her image, responding to a male gaze of greater sophistication with a more rarified "look" (277-279).

Undine is not an 'actress' in the literal sense. Her father's fortune makes this unnecessary, and her upper-class social milieu inadvisable. The stages where she performs are the exclusive dinner parties and social events frequented by Old and New Money. One occasion in particular represents to Undine "her first real taste of life," the perfect "answer to all her wants" (281): dinner hour at the Parisian restaurant "Nouveau Luxe." Here, wealthy Americans and distinguished, but far less prosperous French visitors encounter each other in "a phantom society" (273) that imitates aristocratic codes of conduct, but infuses them with new energy and fresh financial resources. It is this Disney version of aristocracy, rather than a reclusive existence in a remote country seat, however pedigreed, that allows Undine to present herself to greatest advantage, which is her idea of the good life.

But she does not limit herself to the role of an object to be gazed at and consumed by men. Going beyond what Irigaray describes as "speculation," the activity of reflecting men's images back at them, preferably larger than life,[22] she actively "speculates in husbands," as Ammons puts it.[23] The transnational urban space of the "Nouveau Luxe" and the upper-crust drawing rooms of New York thus also serve as 'marketplaces' where Undine acquires her partners, the well-connected Ralph Marvell and later Count Raymond de Chelles. Unlike her father, she cannot make money directly on the stock market. Hence she attempts to achieve similar results by conducting marriage as a business. Occupying both the 'male' and the 'female' position in the gendered exchanges of the marriage market, she "jams the machinery," to use Ellen Dupree's evocative formulation.[24]

This is only possible because divorce no longer results in social exclusion at the end of the nineteenth century. As Debra Ann MacComb points out, contemporary discourses on divorce and "rotary marriage" linked it to "rotary consumption," an emergent cultural pattern in which commodities were replaced before they were used up in response to changing fashions.[25] "[A] contemporary trend in American advertising [...] emphasized the benefits derived from consumption of a product rather than the qualities of the product itself," MacComb explains. "The benefits most often marketed – whether the new product was a car, a washing machine, a dress, or a bread flour – were increased amusement, mobility, freedom and status."[26] In accordance with this logic, Undine discards 'old' husbands for 'the latest model' to improve her social position and to realize the kinds of gains described in the quote.

But despite her expertise, the series of mergers and acquisitions she engineers yields a succession of what David Holbrook calls "unsatisfactory men."[27] Her strategies are thwarted by the fact that her partners possess either superior social and cultural assets or tremendous wealth, but never both. It seems impossible to have the two things she craves – "amusement and respectability" (354) – at the same time.

In the end, Undine settles for financial capital and the importation of European cultural capital. She (re)marries an extremely wealthy American entrepreneur, who presents her with a house on Fifth Avenue that is "an exact copy of the Pitti Palace" in Florence, "a necklace and tiara of pigeon-blood rubies belonging to Queen Marie Antoinette, [and] a million dollar cheque" (586). Symbolically appropriating the social and cultural capital of the Medici and French aristocracy, as well as the seemingly unlimited liquidity of U.S. finance capital, Undine now seems to enjoy the best of both worlds. And yet, Undine's Fifth Avenue mansion is but a simulacrum, and Marie Antoinette's jewelry loses some of its aura as a result of being in the 'wrong place.' Much as the gifts testify to Elmer Moffat's financial potency and the ability of the 'almighty dollar' to reshape cultural landscapes, there is something counterfeit about the cultural capital acquired in this way. Finally, Undine is disappointed because her latest husband cannot secure an Ambassador's post, since the administration does not accept candidates whose wives have been divorced.The novel takes great pains to discredit Undine's ambition and portray it as self-defeating. Whereas she finally opts for money over social capital, it inscribes an Old Money aesthetics that contrasts markedly with her New Money philosophy. However, like Carrie, Undine has successfully challenged gender hierarchies, even from within those institutions designed to uphold them.

Like Dreiser's Carrie, Undine invests her libidinal energies in consumption and self-presentation, rather than her male partners. Relatedly, she refuses the image of the self-sacrificing 'Angel in the House': She wants to be recompensed for her labor not only in love, but also in money. Like any woman who demands to be paid for her work, she is linked to the specter of prostitution, from which only her almost continually married state shields her. If the text does not fully endorse her actions, her portrayal at least raises interesting questions – about gender, consumption, and sex and the city.

4. Conclusions

I would like to return to *Sex and the City* at this point to reflect on the durability of the constellation I have traced in the realist and naturalist texts. The many parallels concerning urban spaces as sites of consumption in the novels published around 1900 and the television series aired almost one hundred years later testify to the persistence of the nexus between gender, sexuality, and economics established in the emergent consumer society of the late nineteenth century. In both cases, department stores, restaurants, and theaters offer opportunities for purchasing material goods and cultural productions; they also allow the female characters to 'shop' for male partners. In this connection, libidinal investments in goods such as clothing do not noticeably differ from feelings for men – if anything, bonds between merchandise and female consumers appear stronger and more passionate than those between heterosexual partners.

While the romance with consumption continues and has even reached new heights with the fetishization of brand names today, the function of the romance script with regard to heterosexual relations has changed markedly. The *literary* characters present themselves as spectacles for the male gaze (not least through the consumption of elegant apparel) as a matter of necessity: Their livelihood depends on it. This is no longer true for the 'career women' in *Sex and the City*, whose economic self-reliance is exemplified by Carrie Meeber's and Kitty Hamilton's success. Their occupations as columnist, PR consultant, or lawyer do not necessarily require their stylization as erotic objects for male consumption. Where a man's attractiveness for Undine, Kitty, and Sister Carrie is directly linked to his earning power, this connection seems to have weakened considerably in the late twentieth century.

One can read this as a sign of progress, as an indication that women's sexual desires can now be expressed more openly, and that the "sexuo-economic relation," as Charlotte Perkins Gilman termed it,[28] has undergone productive revisions. Yet there is something curiously liberating about Undine's and Sister Carrie's lack of interest in heterosexual romance. This becomes visible if one contemplates how the search for 'Mr. Right' dominates the lives of Carrie Bradshaw and her friends (as well as their interaction with each other). They seem no less preoccupied with their looks and with the quest for a heterosexual partnership than their literary forebears.

As sociologist Eva Illouz notes, "love remains one of the most important mythologies of our time."[29] This is due to the fact that romance has assumed many of the functions of religion in secularized Western societies. "Romance took on the properties of *ritual*" in the twentieth century, Illouz writes; "it started drawing on themes and images offering access to a powerful collective utopia of abundance, individualism, and creative self-fulfillment."[30] Perceived as a cornerstone of the 'good life,' romance became inextricable from the notion of the 'American Dream.'[31] For all its utopian potential, though, concepts of romance are gendered – as well as 'raced,' classed, and sexed – in problematic ways. In hegemonic discourses, the ability to find a long-term male lover is still considered the litmus test of a woman's value, while men's worth is not premised on their attractiveness as love objects in the same way.

For the female characters in *Sex and the City*, the centrality of romance translates into their re-subjection to the male gaze and male approval. It is true that they possess a female gaze, too – they consider men as sexual objects in a manner that would have been scandalous only a few decades earlier. If women in patriarchal societies are barred from access to money, the language, and the gaze, as Irigaray argues,[32] their control over financial resources and their ability to look at men as active, desiring subjects indicate important changes in the social order. Their friendship also functions to mitigate the impact of the romance script at least in part. In their professions, the characters wield at least some discursive power.

Still, the political progress they represent is severely limited. Kitty Hamilton and Carrie Meeber mobilize consumption in the service of careers that yield financial independence and at least a measure of creative self-expression. Both achieve popularity and recognition despite being unmarried and, in Kitty Hamilton's case, being targeted by racism. Undine Spragg confounds gender hierarchies by occupying both object and subject position in the marriage market, usurping the male privilege of agency.

Of the *Sex and the City* cast, by contrast, only Samantha Jones remains single, refusing to perform what Susan Maushart calls "wifework." [33] While none of the narratives challenges upper-(middle-) class privilege and ableism, the refusal to address whiteness – in a New York setting, no less – is less palatable today than in Dreiser's and Wharton's novels. While there are clear continuities in the role of the city as a site of female consumption, this might have been politically more productive around 1900 than at the beginning of the twenty-first century.

Notes

[1] Jennifer Scanlon (ed.) (2000). *The Gender and Consumer Culture Reader.* New York: New York University Press, 303-308. Cf. also Juliet B. Schor and Douglas B. Holt (eds.) (2000). *The Consumer Society Reader*. New York: The New Press.
[2] Inderpal Grewal (2005). *Transnational America: Feminisms, Diasporas, Neoliberalisms.* Durham, NC: Duke University Press, 7.
[3] Rachel Bowlby (1985). *Just Looking: Consumer Culture in Dreiser, Gissing and Zola*. New York: Methuen.
[4] Theodore Dreiser (1991 [1900]). *Sister Carrie*. New York: W. W. Norton & Co, 17. Further references to this edition will be included in the text.
[5] Walter Benjamin (1977). *Illuminationen: Ausgewählte Schriften.* Frankfurt a. M.: Suhrkamp, 176 (my translation; E. B.). Cf. also Victoria De Grazia with Ellen Furlough (eds.) (1996). *The Sex of Things: Gender and Consumption in Historical Perspective*. Berkeley: University of California Press.
[6] Bärbel Tischleder (2009). "The Deep Surface of Lily Bart: Visual Economics and Commodity Culture in Wharton and Dreiser." *Amerikastudien/American Studies* 54.1, 67 (59-78).
[7] Philip Fisher (1985). *Hard Facts: Setting and Form in the American Novel*. New York and Oxford: Oxford University Press, 134; cf. 133.
[8] Gail Reekie (1993). *Temptations: Sex, Selling and the Department Store*. St. Leonards, Australia: Allen & Unwin, xiv.

[9] Irene Gammel (1994). *Sexualizing Power in Naturalism: Theodore Dreiser and Frederick Philip Grove*. Calgary: University of Calgary Press, 72.
[10] Jennifer Costello Brezina (2000). "Public Women, Private Acts: Gender and Theater in Turn-of-the-Century American Novels." *Separate Spheres No More: Gender Convergence in American Literature, 1830-1930*. Ed. Monika M. Elbert. Tuscaloosa, AL: The University of Alabama Press, 237 (225-242).
[11] Lawrence R. Rodgers (1992). "Paul Laurence Dunbar's *The Sport of the Gods*: The Doubly Conscious World of Plantation Fiction, Migration, and Ascent." *American Literary Realism* 24.3, 44 (42-53).
[12] Houston A., Jr. Baker (1985). *Blues, Ideology, and Afro-American Literature: A Vernacular Theory*. Chicago: University of Chicago Press, 26-31.
[13] S. M. Miller and Anthony J. Savoie (2002). *Respect and Rights: Class, Race and Gender Today*. Lanham, MD: Rowman & Littlefield, 5.
[14] Paul Laurence Dunbar (1969 [1902]). *The Sport of the Gods*. Miami, FL: Mnemosyne Publishing, 198. Further references included in the text.
[15] Rodgers (1992), 53.
[16] Cf. Evelyn Brooks Higginbotham (1993). *Righteous Discontent: The Women's Movement in the Black Baptist Church, 1880-1920*. Cambridge, MA: Harvard University Press, 185-229; and Claudia Tate (1992). *Domestic Allegories of Political Desire: The Black Heroine's Text at the Turn of the Century*. New York: Oxford University Press.
[17] For an analysis of the continued importance of such stereotypes see bell hooks (1992). *Black Looks: Race and Representation*. Boston: South End, 61-77.
[18] Frances Ellen Watkins Harper (1987 [1892]). *Iola Leroy, or Shadows Uplifted*. Boston: Beacon Press, 256.
[19] *Ibid.*, 219.
[20] Houston A., Jr. Baker (1987). *Modernism and the Harlem Renaissance*. Chicago: Chicago University Press.
[21] Edith Wharton (1956 [1913]). *The Custom of the Country*. New York: Scribner's, 281. Further references to this edition will be included in the text.
[22] Luce Irigaray (1979 [1977]). *Das Geschlecht das nicht eins ist*. Berlin: Merve, 183-184.
[23] Elizabeth Ammons (1980). *Edith Wharton's Argument with America*. Athens: The University of Georgia Press, 121.
[24] Ellen Dupree (1992). "Jamming the Machinery: Mimesis in *The Custom of the Country*." *American Literary Realism* 22.2, 5-16.
[25] Debra Ann MacComb (1996). "New Wives for Old: Divorce and the Leisure-Class Marriage Market in Edith Wharton's *The Custom of the Country*." *American Literature* 68.4, 767-768 (765-797).
[26] *Ibid.*, 768.
[27] David Holbrook (1991). *Edith Wharton and the Unsatisfactory Man*. London: Vision Press/New York: St. Martin's Press.

[28] Charlotte Perkins Gilman (1966 [1898]). *Women and Economics: A Study of the Economic Relation Between Men and Women as a Factor in Social Evolution.* Ed. Carl N. Degler. New York: Harper & Row, 122.
[29] Eva Illouz (1997). *Consuming the Romantic Utopia: Love and the Cultural Contradictions of Capitalism.* Berkeley, CA: University of California Press, 7.
[30] *Ibid.*, 8 (emphasis in the text).
[31] *Ibid.*, 81-111.
[32] Luce Irigaray (1980 [1974]). *Speculum: Spiegel des anderen Geschlechts.* Frankfurt a. M.: Suhrkamp, 185; and Irigaray (1979 [1977]), 31, 185, 211.
[33] Susan Maushart (2002). *Wifework: What Marriage Really Means for Women.* London: Bloomsbury.

Bibliography

Ammons, Elizabeth (1980). *Edith Wharton's Argument with America.* Athens: The University of Georgia Press.

Baker, Houston A., Jr. (1985). *Blues, Ideology, and Afro-American Literature: A Vernacular Theory.* Chicago: University of Chicago Press.

--- (1987). *Modernism and the Harlem Renaissance.* Chicago: Chicago University Press.

Benjamin, Walter (1977). *Illuminationen: Ausgewählte Schriften.* Frankfurt a. M.: Suhrkamp.

Bourdieu, Pierre (1996). *Die feinen Unterschiede: Kritik der gesellschaftlichen Urteilskraft.* Frankfurt a. M.: Suhrkamp.

Bowlby, Rachel (1985). *Just Looking: Consumer Culture in Dreiser, Gissing and Zola.* New York: Methuen.

Brezina, Jennifer Costello (2000). "Public Women, Private Acts: Gender and Theater in Turn-of-the-Century American Novels." *Separate Spheres No More: Gender Convergence in American Literature, 1830-1930.* Ed. Monika M. Elbert. Tuscaloosa: The University of Alabama Press, 225-242.

De Grazia, Victoria, with Ellen Furlough (eds.) (1996). *The Sex of Things: Gender and Consumption in Historical Perspective.* Berkeley: University of California Press.

Dreiser, Theodore (1991 [1900]). *Sister Carrie.* New York: W. W. Norton & Co.

Dunbar, Paul Laurence (1969 [1902]). *The Sport of the Gods.* Miami, FL: Mnemosyne Publishing.

Dupree, Ellen (1992). "Jamming the Machinery: Mimesis in *The Custom of the Country.*" *American Literary Realism* 22.2, 5-16.

Fisher, Philip (1985). *Hard Facts: Setting and Form in the American Novel.* New York and Oxford: Oxford University Press.

Gammel, Irene (1994). *Sexualizing Power in Naturalism: Theodore Dreiser and Frederick Philip Grove*. Calgary: University of Calgary Press.
Gilman, Charlotte Perkins (1966 [1898]). *Women and Economics: A Study of the Economic Relation Between Men and Women as a Factor in Social Evolution*. Ed. Carl N. Degler. New York: Harper & Row.
Grewal, Inderpal (2005). *Transnational America: Feminisms, Diasporas, Neoliberalisms*. Durham, NC: Duke University Press.
Harper, Frances Ellen Watkins (1987 [1892]). *Iola Leroy, or Shadows Uplifted*. Boston: Beacon Press.
Higginbotham, Evelyn Brooks (1993). *Righteous Discontent: The Women's Movement in the Black Baptist Church, 1880-1920*. Cambridge, MA: Harvard University Press.
Holbrook, David (1991). *Edith Wharton and the Unsatisfactory Man*. London: Vision Press/New York: St. Martin's Press.
hooks, bell (1992). *Black Looks: Race and Representation*. Boston: South End.
Illouz, Eva (1997). *Consuming the Romantic Utopia: Love and the Cultural Contradictions of Capitalism*. Berkeley, CA: University of California Press.
Irigaray, Luce (1979 [1977]). *Das Geschlecht das nicht eins ist*. Berlin: Merve.
--- (1980 [1974]). *Speculum: Spiegel des anderen Geschlechts*. Frankfurt a. M.: Suhrkamp.
MacComb, Debra Ann (1996). "New Wives for Old: Divorce and the Leisure-Class Marriage Market in Edith Wharton's *The Custom of the Country*." *American Literature* 68.4, 765-797.
Maushart, Susan (2002). *Wifework: What Marriage Really Means for Women*. London: Bloomsbury.
Miller, S. M., and Anthony J. Savoie (2002). *Respect and Rights: Class, Race and Gender Today*. Lanham, MD: Rowman & Littlefield.
Reekie, Gail (1993). *Temptations: Sex, Selling and the Department Store*. St. Leonards, Australia: Allen & Unwin.
Rodgers, Lawrence R. (1992). "Paul Laurence Dunbar's *The Sport of the Gods*: The Doubly Conscious World of Plantation Fiction, Migration, and Ascent." *American Literary Realism* 24.3, 42-53.
Scanlon, Jennifer (ed.) (2000). *The Gender and Consumer Culture Reader*. New York: New York University Press.
Schor, Juliet B., and Douglas B. Holt (eds.) (2000). *The Consumer Society Reader*. New York: The New Press.
Tate, Claudia (1992). *Domestic Allegories of Political Desire: The Black Heroine's Text at the Turn of the Century*. New York: Oxford University Press.
Tischleder, Bärbel (2009). "The Deep Surface of Lily Bart: Visual Economics and Commodity Culture in Wharton and Dreiser." *Amerikastudien/American Studies* 54.1, 59-78.
Wharton, Edith (1956 [1913]). *The Custom of the Country*. New York: Scribner's.

Contributors' Addresses

Prof. Dr. Eva Boesenberg, Institut für Anglistik und Amerikanistik, Humboldt-Universität, Unter den Linden 6, 10099 Berlin

Professor William Merrill Decker, Department of English, Oklahoma State University, 205 Morrill Hall, Stillwater, OK 74078, USA

Prof. Dr. Katja Kanzler, Institut für Anglistik und Amerikanistik, TU Dresden, Fakultät Sprach-, Literatur- und Kulturwissenschaften, 01062 Dresden

Simone Knewitz, M.A., Institut für Anglistik, Amerikanistik und Keltologie, Universität Bonn, Regina-Pacis-Weg 5, 53113 Bonn

Prof. Dr. Nicole Maruo-Schröder, Institut für Anglistik, Universität Koblenz-Landau, Campus Koblenz, Universitätsstr. 1, 56070 Koblenz

Professor Arthur Redding, Department of English, York University, 208 Stong, 4700 Keele Street, Toronto, Ontario, Canada, M3J 1P3

Prof. Dr. Christoph Ribbat, Institut für Anglistik und Amerikanistik, Universität Paderborn, Warburger Str. 100, 33098 Paderborn

Klara Stephanie Szlezák, MA, American Studies, Universität Regensburg, 93040 Regensburg